christianity
in today's world

second edition

religion
in focus

Other titles in this series

Christianity in today's world TRB 2nd edition ISBN 0 7195 7527 3
Islam in today's world revised edition ISBN 0 7195 7528 1
Islam in today's world TRB ISBN 0 7195 7432 3
Judaism in today's world ISBN 0 7195 7197 9
Judaism in today's world TRB ISBN 0 7195 7433 1

Although every effort was made to ensure that the website addresses were correct at the time of going to press, Hodder Murray cannot be held responsible for the content of any website mentioned in this book.

Papers used in this book are natural, renewable and recyclable products. They are made from wood grown in sustainable forests. The logging and manufacturing processes conform to the environmental regulations of the country of origin.

Orders: please contact Bookpoint Ltd, 130 Milton Park, Abingdon, Oxon OX14 4SB. Telephone: +44 (0)1235 827720. Fax: +44 (0)1235 400454. Lines are open from 9.00a.m. to 6.00p.m., Monday to Saturday, with a 24-hour message answering service. You can also visit our websites www.hoddereducation.co.uk and www.hoddersamplepages.co.uk

Artwork by Conny Jude, Oxford Designers and Illustrators Ltd.
Layouts by Black Dog Design, Buckingham
Cover design by John Townson/Creation
Typeset in 9 on 12pt Stone Serif by Phoenix Photosetting, Chatham, Kent
Printed and bound in Italy

A CIP catalogue record for this book is available from the British Library

ISBN-10: 0 7195 7526 5
ISBN-13: 978 0 7195 7526 6
Teacher's Resource Book ISBN 0 7195 7527 3

christianity
in today's world
second edition

Claire Clinton   Sally Lynch   Janet Orchard
Deborah Weston   Angela Wright

Faith Community editor
Sally Lynch

A MEMBER OF THE HODDER HEADLINE GROUP

ACKNOWLEDGEMENTS

Members of different Christian faith communities have been widely interviewed and consulted in the preparation of this book, although the authors take responsibility for the views expressed herein.

The authors and publishers would like to thank the following for their co-operation:

p.27 Rev Ronald C Purkey; **p.39** Paul and Jane Wells; **p.47** Right Revd John Sentamu; **p.73** Ken Edgar; **p.83** Astrid; **p.84** John Rajah; **p.96** Jonathan Edwards; **p.99** Sarah Bingham; **p.106** pupils at St Bede's Inter-Church Comprehensive School, Cambridge; **p.101** Father Richard Tillbrook.

Written sources

pp.22–3 'Careful death of José' by Dinyar Godrej, *New Internationalist* issue 280, April 1997; **p.27** Article by Deborah Lim, Christian World News. Reprinted with permission of The Christian Broadcasting Network, Inc.. All rights reserved; **p.37** Extract from The Marriage Service in *The Alternative Service Book 1980* © The Central Board of Finance of the Church of England 1980 and is reproduced by permission; **p.51** 'God our Mother' by Janet Morley from *All Desires Known*, SPCK 1992, by permission of SPCK; **p.53** 'Messiah Man' by Ben Okafor from *Racism: whose problem, whose decision?*, Scripture Union; **p.58** abridged from *Building to Share: The Story of John Laing*, by Deborah Helme, Faith in Action series, RMEP, 1998; **p.59** 'Here is a gaping sore' by John L Bell © WGRG, Iona Community, G2 3DH, Scotland, UK; **p.72** 'Creator of Earth' from *Woman Wisdom: A Feminist Lectionary and Psalter: Women of the Hebrew Scriptures, Part One* by Winter, Miriam Therese. Copyright 1991 by Crossroad Publishing Co (NY). Reproduced with permission of Crossroad Publishing Co (NY) in the format Textbook via Copyright Clearance Center; **p.74** from *What the Churches Say*, published by RE Today; **p.90** 'God the Father, God beyond us, we adore you' from *Contemporary Prayers: The Collected Edition*, edited by Caryl Micklem, SCM Press 1993.

Photographs

Cover & p.iii Tony Morrison/South American Pictures; **p.2** *t* & *bl* © Sean Sprague/The Image Works/Topfoto, *c* & *br* ImageWorks/Topfoto; **p.3** *t* © Dave Bartruff/Corbis, *ct* Jerry Bergman/Rex Features, *cb* ImageWorks/Topfoto, *b* Rex Features; **p.11** reproduced courtesy of He Qi www.heqiarts.com; **p.16** *tl* Paul Brown/Rex Features, *tr* Apis Abramis/Alamy, *b* ImageState/Alamy; **p.18** © Reuters/Corbis; **p.21** *t* © Eva-Lotta Jansson/Corbis, *bl* & *br* Dr M.A. Ansary/Science Photo Library; **p.22** © Olivia Rayner; **p.23** Julian Hamilton/Rex Features; **p.25** *l* Rex Features, *r* © Miriam Reik; **p.26** © Sharron Wallace/St Christopher's Hospice; **p.28** Topfoto/National; **p.32** Ark Press; **p.33** Sipa Press/Rex Features; **p.34** courtesy Catholics for a Free Choice; **p.36** *t* Elvele Images/Alamy, *b* © Pete Jones/Photofusion; **p.39** *both* Jane Wells; **p.46** *tl* courtesy Evangelical Alliance, *cl* Michael Booth/Alamy, *bl* Paddy Donnelly/CAFOD, *r* Janine Wiedel Photolibrary /Alamy; **p.47** Stefan Rousseau/PA/Empics; **p.48** *l* © Sonia Halliday Photographs, *tr* Sheffield Galleries and Museums Trust/Bridgeman Art Library, *br* Index/Bridgeman Art Library; **p.49** *tl* © Martin Parr/Magnum Photos, *tr* Rex Features, *bl* © Abbas/Magnum Photos, *bc* Francis Dean/Rex Features, *br* The Board of Trinity College, Dublin, Ireland/ Bridgeman Art Library; **p.50** © Viv Quillin; **p.51** World Religions Photo Library/Alamy; **p.53** *l* © Minn Cooper, *r* © Mike Wells/Aspect Picture Library; **p.54** Window designed by Tom McGuinness and crafted by stained glass artist Edna Partridge and enamel artist Evan Long; **p.55** Andrew Moore/Rex Features; **p.56** *t* Copyright Christian Aid. Used with permission., *b* Christian Aid/Harriet Logan/ Network; **p.57** *tl* & *tr* Copyright Christian Aid. Used with permission., *b* Topfoto; **p.58** *t* courtesy the Laing Family, *b* © Jean-François Cardella/Construction Photography; **p.59** courtesy Iona Community; **p.60** pencil drawing by Ajubel; **p.62** Collection Imperial War Museum, London/ © Janey Webb; **p.64** Jack Barker/Alamy; **p.65** Times Newspapers/ Rex Features; **p.67** *tl* James Fraser/Rex Features, *tr* Reuters/ Damir Sagolj, *b* AP/Wide World Photos; **p.68** *l* © Bernard Bisson/Corbis Sygma, *r* OSPAAL; **p.70** © Luke Warm; **p.72** *t* courtesy Christian Ecology Link (photo: Judith Allinson), *b* photo © Hugh Warwick; **p.73** *both* Janet Orchard; **p.75** *t* Scotsman Publications Ltd, *b* Alan Moir, CWS/CartoonArts International; **p.79** Mount Stromlo and Siding Spring Observatories/Science Photo Library; **p.80** *l* Martin Dohrn/Science Photo Library; **p.81** *l* Sipa Press/Rex Features, *r* © The Natural History Museum, London; **p.83** Jim Belben; **p.84** *both* John Rajah; **p.86** *l to r* artwork by Ellen Horner and Gemma Larkin, St Bede's Comprehensive Church School, Cambridge; **p.87** *l* akg-images/Heiner Heine, *r* Patrick Reyntiens Archive/Bridgeman Art Library; **p.91** *t* Santa Maria Novella, Florence/Bridgeman Art Library, *b* photo © John Crook; **p.93** *l* reproduced courtesy of Corinne Vonaesch, *r* courtesy of Lefevre Fine Art Ltd., London; **p.96** © Sporting Pictures (UK) Ltd; **p.97** Associated Press/Topfoto; **p.98** © Abbas/ Magnum Photos; **p.99** reproduced with the permission of the Library Committee of the Religious Society of Friends; **p.100** *tl* World Religions Photo Library/Alamy, *tr* CIRCA Photo Library, *bl* CIRCA Photo Library/Ged Murray, *br* © Brenda Prince/Photofusion; **p.101** *t* courtesy Richard Tillbrook, *b* John Rajah; **p.104** *l* © Amit Dave/Reuters/Corbis, *r* Joerg Boethling/Still Pictures; **p.105** Baptistry, Florence/ Bridgeman Art Library; **p.106** © Reuters; **p.107** *both* Sally Lynch; **p.110** courtesy of Lefevre Fine Art Ltd., London (photo: Bridgeman Art Library).

t = top, *b* = bottom, *l* = left, *r* = right, *c* = centre

While every effort has been made to contact copyright holders, the publishers apologise for any omissions, which they will be pleased to rectify at the earliest opportunity.

Contents

1.1 INTRODUCTION

What does the Lord's Prayer mean to Christians?

The Lord's prayer is one of the oldest Christian prayers but it is also the most widely used today. It is probably prayed at least a billion times every week around the world. It is a simple prayer but it covers some important ideas of Christianity. Let's find out…

Our Father in Heaven

God is in heaven – way above the human dimension, beyond this world – but at the same time God can also be close to people like a loving parent.

> *Our Father in Heaven*
>
> *May your holy name be honoured*
>
> *May your Kingdom come*
>
> *May your will be done on Earth as it is in Heaven*
>
> *Give us today our daily bread*
>
> *Forgive our sins as we forgive those who sin against us*
>
> *Do not bring us to hard testing*
>
> *But keep us safe from the Evil One*
>
> *For the power and the glory are yours for ever and ever*

May your holy name be honoured

To honour means to worship. Christians worship God in two ways.

- ❏ They try to keep God's commandments in their daily lives. Every time they do God's will they honour God.
- ❏ They also meet with other Christians to sing and pray and praise God.

For the power and the glory are yours for ever and ever

God is eternal. Through their faith Christians believe they can share eternal life with God.

Keep us safe from the Evil One

There is evil in the world. Christians disagree over where it comes from, but they all agree evil must be resisted. **And** they recognise they need God's help and guidance to do this.

May your kingdom come... May your will be done on Earth as it is in Heaven

The Kingdom of God means the rule of God. When God is world ruler there will be justice and fairness for all people. Suffering and sin will be ended. But when...?

- ❑ **...At the end of time?** Some Christians believe God will one day come to rule on Earth. At that time God will defeat all enemies. God will even defeat death itself. God's kingdom will come on Earth.
- ❑ **...Here and now?** Some Christians believe the Kingdom of God is up to us. Human beings bring the Kingdom of God to Earth by living good lives and working and praying for justice.

There are Christians who hold both these beliefs.

Give us today our daily bread

Christians depend on God.

- ❑ Physically because God has provided the perfect world that can feed, clothe, and shelter all people.
- ❑ The bread is also a symbol of spiritual need. God meets their spiritual needs as well. Christians pray for God to feed their souls too. People need this in order to be fully human.

Forgive our sins as we forgive those who sin against us

God sets high standards but God is merciful. Christian people do not live perfect lives. They break God's commandments. But they can turn to God and ask and receive forgiveness and be strengthened by that forgiveness.

There is a condition attached however. To be forgiven by God Christians must also show forgiveness to other people who have sinned against them.

If all the words of the Scriptures were reviewed, you will find nothing, it seems to me, that is not contained or summarised in the 'Our Father'.
St Augustine, fifth century AD

Do not bring us to hard testing

This might sound like Christians are asking for an easy life but that is not what this line means. Christians expect their faith to be tested. They pray that they won't be tested beyond what they can deal with.

DISCUSS

Do you think the Lord's Prayer suggests that being a Christian is easy or hard? Give reasons.

SAVE AS ...

How relevant do you think religious ideas like these are to the world today? Record your views at the beginning of this course. Be specific if you can – comment on at least one of the beliefs described on this page.

Later in this book after you have explored how Christians apply their beliefs to some issues facing them in the modern world, you will see if your views have changed at all.

1.3

PERSONAL
ETHICS

How do *you* make moral decisions?

Morality is the study of right and wrong. To start thinking about how Christians make moral decisions, you are going to look at how *you* make them.

What would you do if . . . ?

ACTIVITY

Here are four everyday dilemmas. What do you think is right and wrong in these situations? And how do you decide?

Work in pairs. Consider each dilemma in turn.

1 What do you think is the 'right' thing for the person to do in this situation? Explain why you think it is right.
2 What do you think is the 'wrong' thing? Explain why you think it is wrong.
3 Explain what you would do if you were in that situation.
4 List the factors that would affect your decision if you were in that situation.
5 When everyone has considered at least two dilemmas, as a class, make a list of the factors that affected people's decisions.

Dilemma 1: The £20 note

I never have as much money as my friends. My mum is so tight with her money. I don't have as many clothes, CDs or treats as everyone else. They all go out more than I do and their parents always pay for them.

One day I got home from school a bit earlier than usual. Mum was still at work. I noticed that she had left a £20 note in the kitchen. I thought of all the things that I could do with the money ...

Should she:
Take the money
or
Leave it where it is
or
... ?

Dilemma 2: The lousy school report

I'm always getting into trouble at school. The teachers are always getting at me. The homework is too hard and takes too long. Other people get their parents to help them but my dad won't help me. I don't think he can do it either, but he won't admit it.

I've got my end of year report in my bag to take home to my dad. It's really bad. He'll kill me when he reads it. I'm in trouble ...

Should he:
Hide the report
or
Show the report to his dad
or
... ?

DISCUSS

1 Not all decisions are moral decisions. Do you think the following are moral decisions or not?

a) what to have for breakfast

b) who to choose as your boyfriend or girlfriend

c) whether to shop at your local corner shop or Tesco

d) which football team to support

e) whether to give money to Comic Relief

f) whether to travel to school by car or bus

g) whether to have an abortion.

Give reasons for your answers.

2 How do *you* decide between right and wrong?

- Do you ask advice from other people?
- Do you think of what your religion or upbringing has taught you?
- Do you think, 'What would so-and-so do in this situation?' and try to follow some example?
- Do you work out an answer for yourself? For example, do you think, 'What would happen if I …' and go for the option with the best outcome?

SAVE AS …

3 Keep a moral dilemma diary for a few days. Note down every time you face a moral dilemma – a situation where you feel you have to decide between right and wrong.
Note possible courses of action, the decision you take, and why.

Dilemma 3: The new boyfriend

My family is very strict. As soon as school finishes I am expected to go straight home. One time a teacher kept me behind for a detention without telling my parents. My dad was furious. He came up to school and shouted at the people in the office. I felt really embarrassed.

Now I've met this boy I really like. Dad will disapprove so the only way I can meet him is to sneak out of school to meet him in the park. I've already been caught once. If it happens again they said they would tell my dad. I don't know what my dad will do if he finds out …

Should she:
Give up her boyfriend
or
Keep on seeing her boyfriend in secret
or
… ?

Dilemma 4: The invitation

There's this group in my class who go out at weekends and have a good time and get really drunk. I get on OK with them and I've been asked to go along. I'd like to, it would be great for my image, but I'm not sure I should. I don't think my parents would care. They go out themselves every Friday and Saturday. And I'm 15, almost an adult …

Should he:
Go out drinking with his friends
or
Find something else to do on Friday and Saturday nights
or
… ?

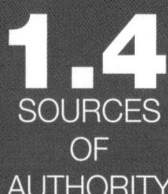

How do Christians make moral decisions?

Making moral decisions is a bit like steering a ship through dangerous or exciting unknown waters. To help you reach a decision you are happy about and that you feel is right there are 'islands' you can visit. These islands are your 'sources of moral authority'. Over the next six pages you will find out more about Christian 'sources of authority'. At the end you should be able to chart a Christian route across the Moral Ocean.

✓ CHECKPOINT

Sources of moral authority for Christians

Different Christian traditions favour different routes through the Moral Ocean. For example:

- Evangelical Christians emphasise that God's guidance can be found in the inspired words of *the Bible*.
- Catholic and Orthodox Christians emphasise how the *official teachings of their Church* can also guide Christians.
- Many Christians from all traditions find that their own *reason* and the *advice of other people*, such as Christian leaders, writers or friends, can guide them.
- Most stress the role of *individual conscience* in making moral decisions.
- All Christian traditions see Jesus' life as a source of moral authority. Jesus is called 'the Word of God' by one of the New Testament writers. It is as if *Jesus' words and actions* show how God wants Christians to behave. Many Christians therefore ask: 'What would Jesus do in this situation?' and try to follow this example.

Pages 8–11 explore these in more detail.

WHAT SHALL I DO?

Parents

Conscience

Family

Jesus

Local priest or minister

✔ CHECKPOINT

You will need to know the meaning of these two terms:

- **absolute morality** – this is when a person believes that there is a right course of action in a moral dilemma that is true in all situations, regardless of culture, religious tradition, time or age. For example: 'it is always wrong to kill'.
- **relative morality** – this is when a person has strong beliefs or principles but they believe that different courses of action might be needed in different situations. For example: 'it is usually wrong to kill, but sometimes it might be necessary for a particular reason.'

SAVE AS ...

Throughout this book you will be investigating examples of people who have taken absolutist or relativist stances. Draw up a table with three columns:

- issue
- absolutist example(s)
- relativist example(s).

As you work through this book you can use it to record examples of each approach.

🔍 FOCUS TASK

This illustration shows some factors that might influence some people when they are making a moral decision.

Stage 1

1 You are trying to make up your mind on some big issue. You can call at five islands before making your final decision. Which will they be? On your own copy of this picture, mark your route. If we have missed off some of your favoured sources of moral authority, you can add and label other islands.
2 Write an explanation of your route. Include your ideas about what your choices say about you.

Stage 2

After you have studied the next four pages return to your chart and plot the route that might be taken by a Christian. You can find more advice about this on page 11.

The Ten Commandments – Principles for behaviour

A moral code is a set of principles that help to guide your decisions. Most people would recognise the famous part of the Christian moral code, 'The Ten Commandments'. These were originally given to the Israelites over 3000 years ago and they are still widely respected and used today.

The first four commandments focus on how to worship God.

The remaining six are about how to live peaceably with other people in society.

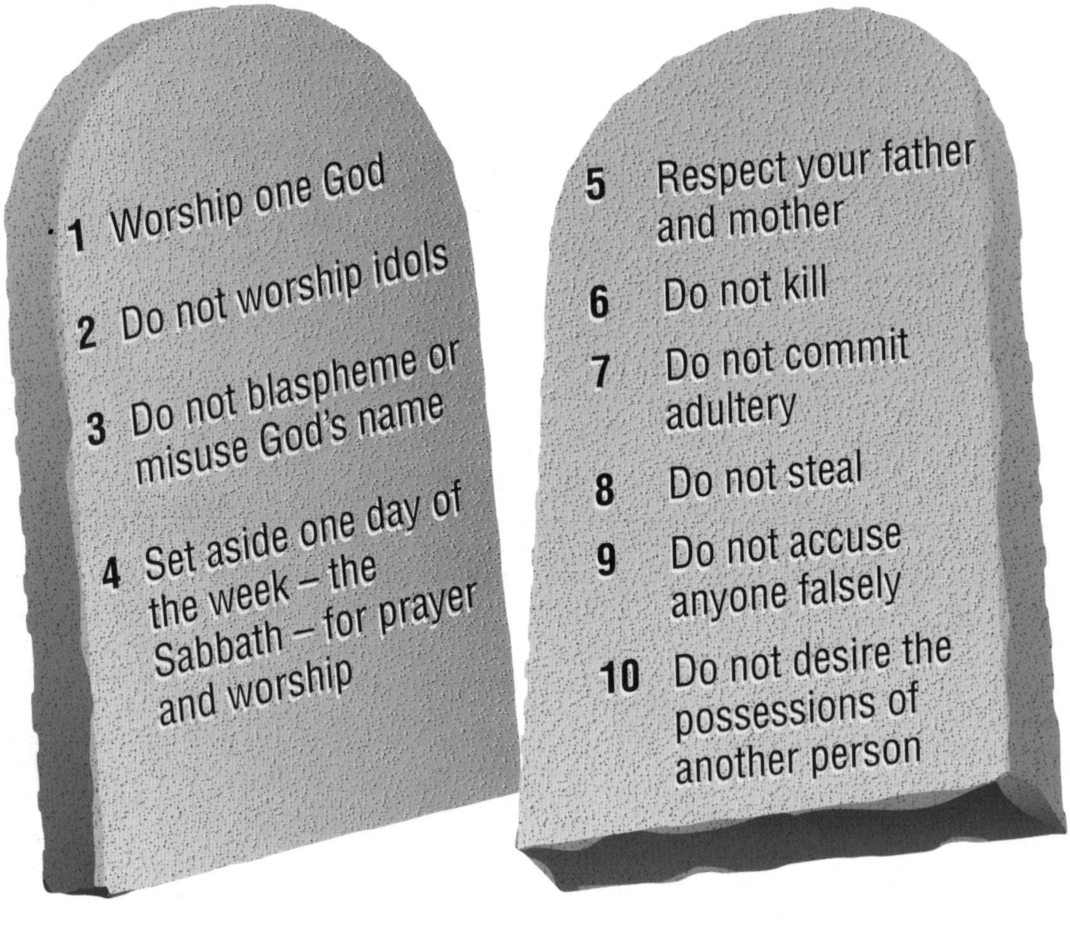

1 Worship one God

2 Do not worship idols

3 Do not blaspheme or misuse God's name

4 Set aside one day of the week – the Sabbath – for prayer and worship

5 Respect your father and mother

6 Do not kill

7 Do not commit adultery

8 Do not steal

9 Do not accuse anyone falsely

10 Do not desire the possessions of another person

These were not easy commands to follow. The Old Testament is full of stories of people struggling to apply these rules in complex situations.

DISCUSS

1 Think about an issue covered in the newspapers, local and national, over the past week where one or more of these commandments are being broken.

2 Look for examples, or imagine your own, in which people today are still keeping to these commandnents.

3 Do you think that any of these commandments are no longer relevant in today's world? Be prepared to justify your answer.

ACTIVITY

4 Imagine you have the opportunity to replace one of these commandments with a new one.

a) As a class brainstorm possible extras then take a vote to see which is the most popular.

b) Try to agree which of the original ten you would take away to make space for your new one.

Jesus and the Great Commandments – Law versus love

The Ten Commandments were still the main guide to moral behaviour for all Jews during Jesus' lifetime. To help people apply the commandments fairly and consistently in everyday life, many other laws and regulations had been added. Where the Ten Commandments explain a simple principle 'Do not commit adultery', the later laws stated what the penalty for adultery should be within society. These laws changed and adapted over time.

Jesus said he had not come to do away with these laws but to help people keep them. So he summed them up in a much simpler moral code: **Two Great Commandments** that summarise in two simple phrases the spirit of the whole Law of God.

A

'In our law Moses commanded that such a woman must be stoned to death. Now what do you say?' They said this to trap Jesus.

(John 8.5–6)

Woman caught in adultery by He Qi

❑ *'**Love the Lord your God** with all your heart, with all your soul, and with all your mind.'* This is the greatest and the most important commandment.

❑ *The second most important commandment is like it:* '**Love your neighbour as you love yourself.**' *The whole Law of Moses and the teachings of the prophets depend on these.*
Matthew 22.37–40

According to Jesus, people who worship God **and** act lovingly towards others are doing God's will. This approach to moral decision-making was different from what had gone before. Instead of finding a law and applying it rigidly Jesus called on people to act in a loving way even if that meant ignoring the law.

For example, some Pharisees brought to Jesus a woman who had committed adultery (Source A). The Law said she should be stoned and the Pharisees wanted to see what Jesus would do. You can find out what he did in John 8.1–11. His solution combined subtlety, forgiveness and compassion. Jesus did not **want** people to disobey the Law. But he did want them to balance the demands of the Law with compassion and love.

Many Christians today regard Jesus – what he did and what he said in this kind of situation – as their greatest source of moral authority. When faced with a new situation they think about what Jesus would do.

DISCUSS

1 Read the story of the woman caught in adultery in John 8.1–11. Explain in your own words, using the two great commandments as a guide, why you think Jesus took the course of action he did.
2 Do you personally think his actions were justified?
3 Do the same with the story of Jesus healing on the Sabbath found in Mark 3.1–5.
4 Describe a situation in the modern world where love and law might be in conflict. What do you think Jesus might do in this situation? Why?

SAVE AS...

Jesus taught a lot about how to love God and to love your neighbour. The most famous collection of Jesus' teachings about human relationships is found in the Sermon on the Mount in Matthew chapters 5 to 7. Using your Bibles or the sheet your teacher can give you, record one thing that Jesus taught about each of the following:

a) Adultery and divorce
b) Judging others
c) Love for enemies
d) Giving money and praying
e) Wealth and possessions.

The Bible – God's word for all time?

Sacred texts are important in most religions. The Bible is the most sacred text for Christian believers and an absolutely vital source of authority. The Bible gives all Christians access to the great teachings that reveal what God wants.

CHECKPOINT

How to use the Bible in your exam

For your exam you will be expected to include quotations from the Bible to support your answers. In fact if you don't quote from the Bible you will not be able to get top marks however clever your answers are in other ways.

So throughout this book we have included key texts relating to each issue. Getting to know them is built into the main activities. Your teacher can also give you some Bible file cards that summarise key passages for your revision.

However, don't confuse the way the examiner wants you to use the Bible and the way that most Christians actually use it in daily life. For Christians the Bible is not a collection of short sayings – Christians don't look for the one-liner that says it all. They don't live their lives by single verses. Rather they look for the underlying principles. These verses are only important because they **sum up** a key principle.

So in your exam, when you quote the Bible, don't say things like:

Christians believe that life is sacred because the 6th commandment says 'You shall not kill'.

Instead you need to recognise that this is just one example of a principle that Christians believe runs through the whole of the Bible. So instead you should say things like:

Christians believe that life is sacred. The Bible supports this view in many ways, for example the 6th commandment says 'you shall not kill'.

It may seem like a small difference to you but it shows that you understand.

The Old Testament

❏ The first five books (**the Pentateuch**) focus on the Ten Commandments and the Law of Moses.
❏ **The Writings and the Prophets** tell the 1500-year-long story of the people of Israel trying to apply God's law in the real world.

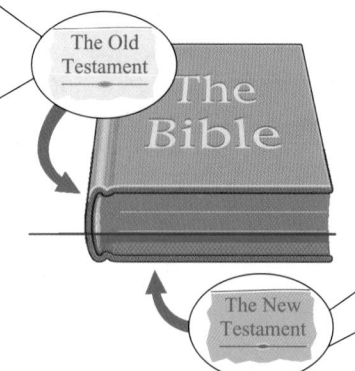

The New Testament

❏ **The Gospels** recount the life of Jesus.
❏ **Acts and the Letters** tell the story of Jesus' followers trying to follow the example of Jesus in the real world.

God's words or human words?

All Christians would agree that the Bible is important. However Christians disagree as to what kind of book it is.

An evangelical perspective

I believe that the Bible is the **timeless**, and **inspired** Word of God. It is as relevant today as it was hundreds of years ago. I believe that the writing of the Bible was actually inspired by God – the writers were writing what God wanted them to write. It is God's words. So I can read the Bible and hear directly what God wants me to hear.

A liberal perspective

I believe the Bible does reveal God's wishes and desires for the world but that these are often **mysterious**. The truth of the Bible, rather like poetry, is revealed through symbols, metaphors and similes and not through the literal meaning of every word.

I also believe that the people who wrote it were from a **particular time and place**. Sometimes they said things that reflected the particular values of the day rather than the mind of God, for instance telling slaves to 'obey their masters'. So I always try to look for the key principles in the Bible and apply those rather than the particular examples.

Church teachings – God's word for the modern world?

Nearly all Christians would accept the Bible as a source of authority but some would balance it against the teachings and traditions of the Church. Many moral issues in the modern world, including some that you will study in this course, were not issues at all in the time of the Bible. So to find guidance on them from the Bible means looking for principles and then applying those. In some traditions this is left up to the **individual**. In other traditions – particularly in the Catholic tradition – it is the role of the **leaders of the Church**, particularly the Pope, to work out teachings that should be followed by all Catholics.

This is a **practical approach** when difficult decisions have to be made. The view is that if the great minds in the Catholic Church spend time thinking through an issue, praying about it, reading what the Bible has to say and discussing it with others, they are more likely to come out with sensible and godly answers than individual Christians or groups of ordinary Christians thinking it through on their own with just the Bible to guide them.

For this reason Catholics believe that the **writings of saints**, **other leaders** and **decisions made by leaders** in the Councils of the Church are all a source of authority for individual Christians around the world. You can find an example of how the Catholic Church works out its teachings on page 97.

In Protestant Churches, such as the Church of England, the leaders do the same things – they meet and discuss and read the Bible and pray together about any issue, and they make pronouncements, but **they do not usually regard their decisions as compulsory** for ordinary Church members. They are much more likely to suggest their findings are a guide for ordinary believers. The individual then has to decide what to do or how to behave.

ACTIVITY

1 Look at the following statements. Do you think they would be most likely to be said by an evangelical or a liberal? Give reasons.

> 1 The Bible can never be wrong, on anything. God can't make mistakes.

> 2 God should have put a disclaimer on the front of every Bible – the views expressed are the opinions of the individual writer and are not necessarily the official divine view.

> 3 The Bible really confuses me. Some of it seems so relevant. Some of it is just so irrelevant.

2 Here are two more statements. Which one is more likely to be said by a Catholic? Give your reasons.

> 4 Whatever I do, I look for guidance in the Bible before I do it.

> 5 The Bible is important but not as important as what my church leaders say.

3 Choose which one of the five statements you most agree with. If you agree with none of them, write a statement to sum up your own view of the Bible.

FOCUS TASK

1 On page 7 you charted your own path across the moral ocean. Now it is time to go back to that chart and to think about how a Christian person might cross that ocean. On your own copy of the chart plot their route. They can only visit five islands. Make sure they visit their most important island first. You may want to label the empty island or add more islands if you need to.

If you think there might be a difference between the route that might be taken by different Christians use different colours to mark the routes.

2 What differences, if any, are there between the Christian route and the route that you might take?

SAVE AS…

3 You might want to revise your ideas further as you work through this book. But once you have a route you think is correct write your own explanation of what this tells you about the way that Christians make moral decisions.

2.1
Sanctity of life

In this unit you are going to study two issues: abortion and euthanasia. But first of all you will examine some key beliefs of Christians that affect their attitudes to both issues.

 ## KEY CHRISTIAN BELIEFS: All life is sacred...

Most people feel that life is valuable. But Christianity teaches that every person is made in God's image and all life is a gift from God and is therefore sacred. The diagram below summarises what this means.

 ## FOCUS TASK

1 Make your own copy of this 'cell' diagram.
2 Look at the Bible references below. These are verses from the Bible that some Christians would use to support the ideas in the diagram.
3 Write each Bible reference alongside the idea which it supports. Add your explanation of how it supports this idea. You might feel some of the passages can be used to support more than one idea.
4 Across the bottom of your diagram write your own short caption summarising what Christians mean by 'the sanctity of life'.
5 Use your finished diagram and caption to create a poster called 'The sanctity of life'.

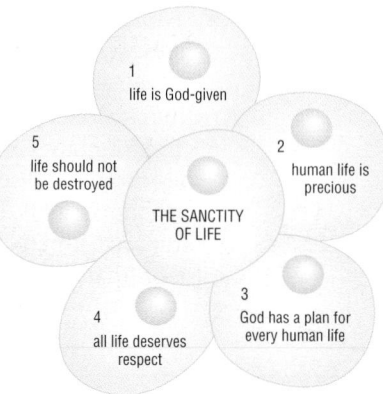

1 life is God-given

5 life should not be destroyed

THE SANCTITY OF LIFE

2 human life is precious

4 all life deserves respect

3 God has a plan for every human life

A
Psalm 139.13–16
You created every part of me;
you put me together in my mother's womb.
I praise you because you are to be feared;
all you do is strange and wonderful.
I know it with all my heart.
When my bones were being formed,
carefully put together in my mother's womb,
when I was growing there in secret,
you knew that I was there –
you saw me before I was born.
The days allotted to me
had all been recorded in your book,
before any of them ever began.

B
Luke 12.6–7
'Aren't five sparrows sold for two pennies? Yet not one sparrow is forgotten by God. Even the hairs of your head have all been counted. So do not be afraid; you are worth much more than many sparrows!'

C Exodus 20.13 (the sixth commandment)
Do not commit murder.

D
1 Corinthians 3.16–17
Surely you know that you are God's temple and that God's Spirit lives in you! So if anyone destroys God's temple, God will destroy him. For God's temple is holy, and you yourselves are his temple.

E
Genesis 1.27
So God created human beings, making them to be like himself. He created them male and female.

... and death is not the end

A

Death is not a full stop, it's a comma. If you look at the whole of life, death is an activity in the middle. It is not an end.

Christian writer and actress Ellen Wilkie, who throughout her life suffered from incurable muscular dystrophy

Most Christians believe there is life after death although there are different ideas about what this means. Some believe in a physical resurrection – their bodies will rise again and go to heaven, just as Jesus did. Others believe in the immortality of the soul – the soul lives on after the body dies. There is a lot more on Christian beliefs about life after death on pages 108–111 but here we are just interested in one key idea that follows from this:

'Death comes at the appointed time'

Just as God has a plan for when life begins and a plan for each person's life, so God also has a plan for when that life should end. It is not in human power to decide when someone should die.

Key questions for Christians

The sanctity of life is a core principle for Christians. However, applying that principle in the real world raises difficult questions as you can see from the diagram below.

B

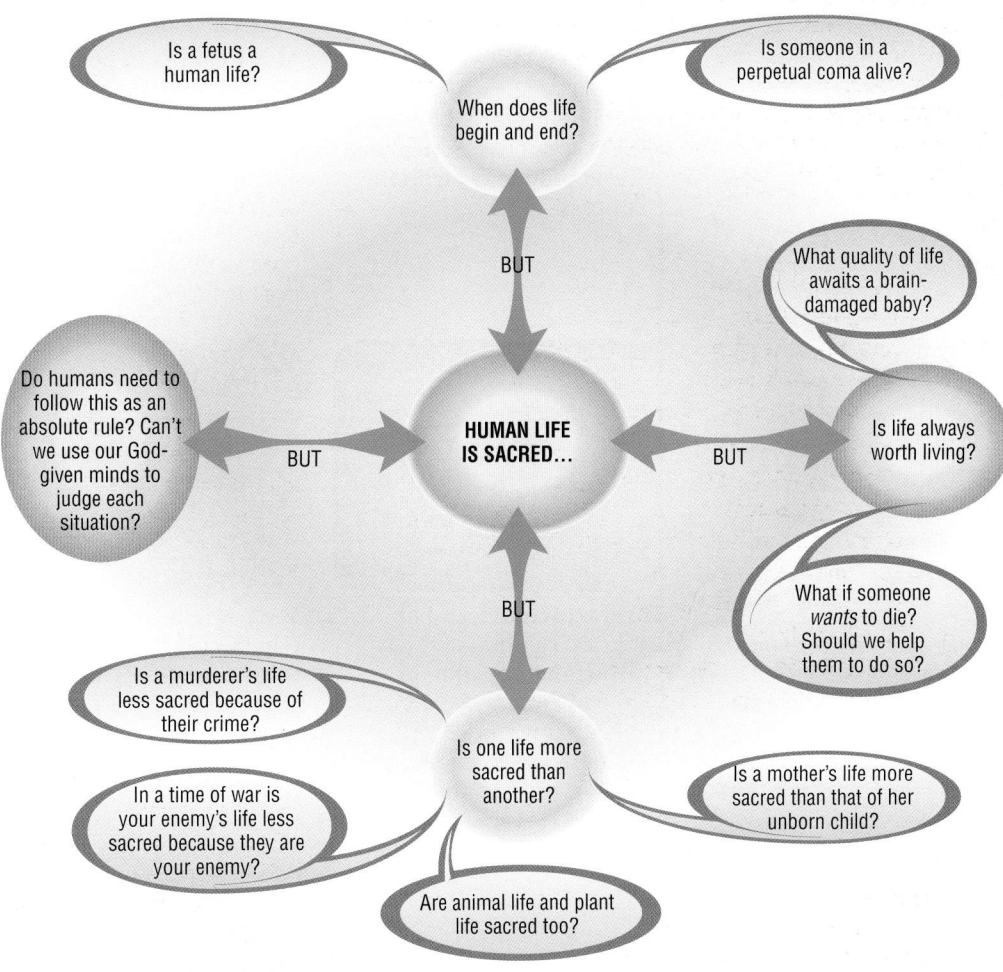

- Is a fetus a human life?
- Is someone in a perpetual coma alive?
- When does life begin and end?
- BUT
- What quality of life awaits a brain-damaged baby?
- Do humans need to follow this as an absolute rule? Can't we use our God-given minds to judge each situation?
- BUT
- **HUMAN LIFE IS SACRED...**
- BUT
- Is life always worth living?
- What if someone *wants* to die? Should we help them to do so?
- BUT
- Is a murderer's life less sacred because of their crime?
- In a time of war is your enemy's life less sacred because they are your enemy?
- Is one life more sacred than another?
- Is a mother's life more sacred than that of her unborn child?
- Are animal life and plant life sacred too?

✔ CHECKPOINT

For your exam you will need to know the meaning of the term SANCTITY OF LIFE. This is the belief that life is holy or sacred. You will need to be able to understand how Christians apply it to different moral issues. It reappears in the investigations into abortion (2.2), euthanasia (2.3), and the environment (5.4) as well as wealth and poverty (5.2) and war and peace (5.3).

DISCUSS

Study Diagram B. In pairs choose one of the key questions in the bubbles which interests you. You are going to debate this topic for one minute. One of you will speak for Yes, the other No (whatever your actual viewpoint is).

Why do many Christians oppose abortion?

Abortion has been legal in Britain for more than 35 years. But some Christians would say that making something legal doesn't make it morally right. In this investigation you will find out what Christians believe about abortion and why. You will also try out a moral issue writing frame, which should be useful throughout your course.

✓ CHECKPOINT

Abortion law in Britain
Since 1968 abortion has been legal in Britain if:

- two doctors agree that it is needed
- it is carried out on registered premises
- the baby is not yet capable of surviving. (The legal term is 'viable' – this means 'able to survive apart from the mother if born and cared for medically'.)

In deciding if an abortion is needed, doctors must consider whether:

a) the life or physical health of the mother is at risk
b) her mental health is at risk
c) an existing family will suffer if the pregnancy continues
d) there is a reasonable chance that the child will be born seriously disabled.

In cases b) and c) the latest termination date is 24 weeks. There is no time limit in case a) or d).

The number of abortions rose steadily to start with, but the number has declined since the early 1990s. Most abortions now take place in the first 12 weeks of pregnancy. Some people say that in Britain there is effectively 'abortion on demand'. Some would even say that abortion is now treated as a form of contraception.

⟶ STARTER

Sammi is 16 years old, about to start her GCSE year, and has just discovered that she is seven weeks pregnant. She doesn't know who the father is.

Mrs Perry is in her thirties. She is a practising Christian. She is married. She is pregnant with her first child. She has just been told that a scan shows her 22-week-old fetus will almost certainly be born with a severe physical disability.

Mrs Oldfield is in her thirties. Her husband has just left her for another woman and moved abroad. She is left with two children under ten years of age. To her surprise, she finds she is 12 weeks pregnant with her estranged husband's baby.

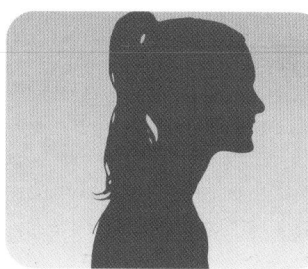

Ms X is in her twenties. She is ten weeks pregnant with twins. She already has one child. She and her partner would like just one more child. She is considering 'selective abortion'. Doctors can inject one fetus to kill it. This endangers the life of both babies but if it succeeds, the dead fetus shrivels up and the remains are born with the placenta at full term.

DISCUSS
Work in groups.

1 For each example discuss:
   a) What action should the person take immediately?
   b) What factors should the person consider in deciding whether to ask for an abortion?
   c) Should each person be allowed an abortion?

What support or help will the person need?

Use the Checkpoint to help you.

2 Look again at the case of Ms X. This is a real case, which caused a storm of protest when the story appeared in the press. Do you think that aborting one twin is morally different from:
   a) aborting a single fetus
   b) aborting both twins?

Give your reasons.

SAVE AS …

3 Write a letter to one of the women, telling her your views on her situation. Include:
   a) how the law applies to her situation
   b) what you would advise her to do.

KEY CHRISTIAN BELIEFS: Abortion

Abortion is not mentioned in the Bible but, from its earliest history, the Church has consistently opposed it.

DISCUSS

1 What does the phrase 'lesser of two evils' mean? How can it be applied to the issue of abortion?

SAVE AS...

2 Record these examples of absolutist and relativist morality on the chart you began on page 9.

Fourth century

Thou shalt not slay thy child by causing abortion, nor kill that which is already born, for everything that has been shaped by and has received a soul from God, if it is slain, shall be avenged.

From the Apostolic Constitution, written in the fourth century CE

Sixteenth century

Abortion is worse than killing a man in his own home.

John Calvin, a leading Protestant theologian, 1509–64

This remained the attitude of most Christians until the 1960s.

Twentieth century

PRO-LIFE OR ANTI-ABORTION

Some Christians, particularly those in the Catholic Church, maintained the Church's traditional teaching.

A

Abortion has been considered to be murder since the first centuries of the Church, and nothing permits it to be considered otherwise.

Pope Paul VI speaking in 1970

This has remained the teaching of the Catholic Church. Here is what Cardinal Hume, the then leader of the Catholic Church in Britain, had to say in 1997:

B

Abortion is a great evil. Abortion was legalised in this country thirty years ago this weekend. It is a great scandal that since 1967 nearly 5 million abortions have taken place. As a nation we should all hang our heads in shame.

Why is abortion a great evil? Because it destroys human life. Human life is a gift of God. It is sacred. Human life is to be respected and protected from the moment of conception to its natural end.

Cardinal Hume

Cardinal Hume believed that abortion was wrong whatever the situation, even, for example, when a pregnancy is the result of a rape. This view is an example of **absolute morality** – one rule for all situations.

PRO-CHOICE

Some Christians reached a different conclusion. They thought that abortion should be made legal.

Partly they were influenced by what was going on in the real world. There were up to 200,000 illegal abortions taking place every year. These were performed by unqualified people in unregistered premises in unhealthy conditions. Yet thousands of women every week were so unhappy about being pregnant that they were prepared to pay a lot of money and risk their lives to have an abortion.

Some Christians argued that in this situation abortion was the 'lesser of two evils'. David Steel, the MP who brought the Abortion Bill to parliament, was himself a Christian. His bill was supported by the leader of the Anglican Church – the Archbishop of Canterbury. These Christians did not reject the idea of sanctity of life, but they weighed it against other principles from the Bible.

❑ **Love:** the most loving behaviour towards the mother might be to allow her to have a safe abortion.
❑ **Free will:** a woman should have some say over what happens to her own body.

Pro-choice Christians leave it to individuals to decide whether abortion is right or wrong for them. They feel it is impossible to make rules that apply in all situations, and that individuals are best placed to make difficult moral decisions such as whether to have an abortion. This is an example of **relative morality** – different rules for different situations.

To be pro-choice does not mean to be pro-abortion. Many pro-choice Christians would see abortion as a last resort. They tolerate abortion rather than favouring it.

VIEWPOINTS: Abortion

C

Abortion is always a tragedy, both in the life which is destroyed and in the health of the mother. It should never be used as a method of birth control.

Tearfund population policy. Tearfund is an evangelical Christian organisation working in developing countries.

D

'Have the baby,' they say. 'Someone will help you.' But where is the support when the mother has a screaming two-year-old, no money and feels like she hasn't a friend in the world? Motherhood is a lifelong commitment – a life of denying yourself and putting your child first – not to be entered into lightly. Adoption is no cosy alternative. It is deeply traumatic for the mother and the child.

A Christian who works in fostering and adoption

E

In July 1997 the first baby was born to a 15-year-old mother under a new scheme started by the Catholic Church in Scotland. Mothers who choose to have their baby rather than an abortion receive money for clothes and equipment.
  The scheme gets three enquiries per day from mothers who are deciding between abortion and continuing their pregnancy.

Description of the Pro-Life Initiative, started by the late Cardinal Winning.

F

Are we sure, on biblical grounds, that it is always the just and loving thing to bring into this demanding complex world a badly deformed, perhaps even mentally incomplete individual? … While the Bible establishes the 'sanctity of life', the stress of the Bible is on 'quality of life'.

L. Kalland in *Abortion, Can an Evangelical Consensus be Found?*

G

James Kopp, on trial for the murder of an abortion doctor in Canada. Kopp is a devout Roman Catholic. He claims it was his religious calling to fire a high-powered assault rifle at an abortion doctor to protect children scheduled to be aborted. He had not intended to kill the doctor, just to injure him as a warning. He feels it 'consistent with his Catholic faith' to take up arms against abortion providers.

H

To have a child is a sacred choice; to not have a child is a sacred choice. Government has no business interfering with a woman who struggles with that choice with her doctor and, more importantly, with her God.

Rev. Carlton Veazey, a Baptist minister in the USA and president of the Religious Coalition for Reproductive Choice (quoted by Miriam Markovitz in *American Prospect* 2003)

I

The greatest destroyer of peace in the world today is abortion. If a mother can kill her own child, what is there to stop you and me from killing each other? The only one who has the right to take life is the one who created it [God].
  It is only our hearts that are not big enough… If there is a child you don't want or can't feed or educate, give that child to me. I will not refuse any child.
  We are fighting abortion by adoption and have given thousands of children to caring families.

Mother Teresa, a Catholic nun, in a letter to the UN Population Conference, 1994

ACTIVITY

Study Sources C–I.

1 Divide them into pro-choice/ pro-life/not sure.
2 List the arguments for and against abortion used in the sources.
3 Which source do you think takes the most loving or compassionate approach? Give reasons.

ACTIVITY

Work in pairs. Look at this unfinished story strip. Your task is to complete two versions of it. One of you show how the story might finish if the website Sammi goes to is run by pro-life Christians. The other should show how it might end if it is run by pro-choice Christians. Remember that:

- pro-life Christians take an absolutist stance that abortion is wrong, although they cannot force anyone to take their advice.
- pro-choice Christians take a relativist stance, according to the circumstances of the mother-to-be.

Try to incorporate as many of the ideas on pages 16–18 as you can.

Sammi finds out she is pregnant.

She talks to her friends.

She prays.

She looks on the internet.

Sammi finds a website.

FOCUS TASK

In your exam you may be asked to write an essay about an issue. This is quite easy as long as you've done your revision and you know how to structure your essay.

Paragraph 1 – Explain what the issue is, including the legal position in this country. Define any key terms. This shows the examiner you are confident of what you know.

Paragraph 2 – Explain what one tradition believes. Include a reference to a sacred text or a church teaching.
   Present this fairly. Don't give your view yet.

Paragraph 3 – Explain the contrasting viewpoint. Again include a sacred text or teaching. Be fair.
   These two paragraphs show that you know there are two sides to the question.

Paragraph 4 – This is where you can speak your mind. Be brief. Don't repeat the arguments again. Just focus on your view and on at least one reason for it.

Now use this formula to write an essay: 'Why do many Christians oppose abortion?' In paragraphs 2 and 3 try to include the following religious principles in your answer:

a) sanctity of life
b) quality of life
c) compassion
d) free will.

⊙ ISSUE 1: When does life begin?

One difference between pro-life and pro-choice Christians is over when life begins. The Catholic Church nowadays argues that life begins at conception. Some other Christians take a different view.

J

From the time that the egg is fertilised, a life has begun which is neither that of the father nor of the mother. It is rather the life of a new human being with all its own growth. It would never be made human if it were not already human.

From the Catholic Declaration on Procured Abortion, 1974

K

...at this earliest stage of their existence, embryos do not have the moral value of persons. They are to be treated with respect; but essentially they are no different from the product of early miscarriages, and the way these have usually been handled is the best guide to what to do.

Lord Habgood, former Anglican Archbishop of York

ACTIVITY

Your teacher will give you a copy of Chart L. You will need coloured pens and pencils.

1. Mark in one colour the point on the arrow when you think life begins.
2. Mark in another colour the period when abortion is legal in Britain. Refer to the Checkpoint on page 16.
3. Use a third colour to mark the period when you think abortion should be legal. If you think abortion should never be legal, draw a line at Week 0.
4. Mark with a fourth colour the time at which you think the fetus develops a spirit or a soul. If you do not believe in spirits or souls, do not draw this line.
5. If you have allowed for a spirit or a soul, mark on the diagram of the fetus the place where you think the soul is. Discuss this if you find it difficult.
6. Add a key to explain the significance of all the colours.
7. Write a thought bubble saying how you feel about this activity.

L

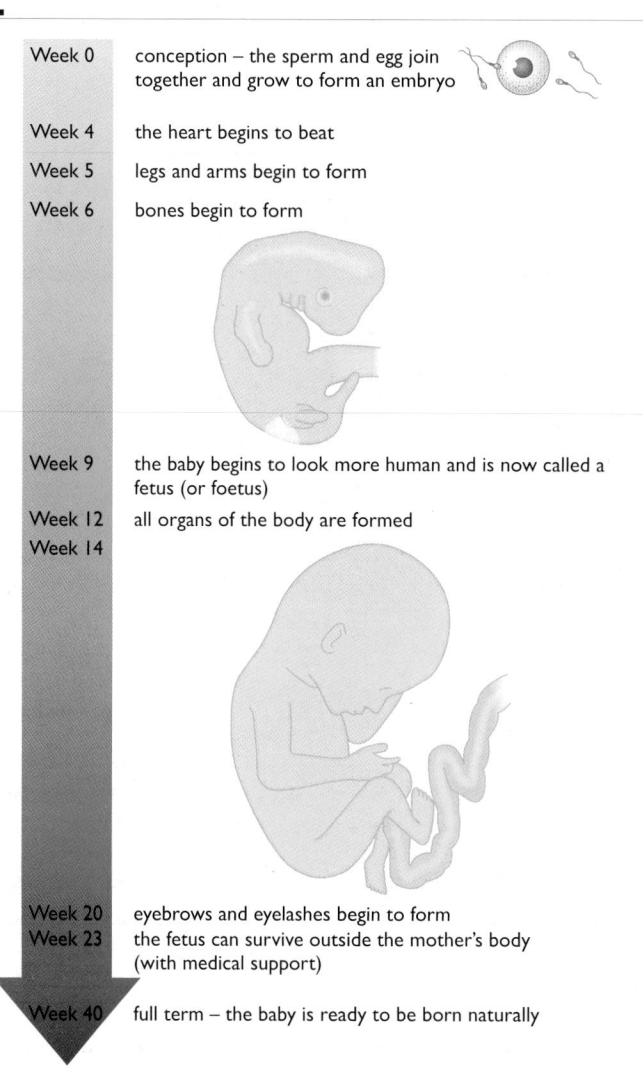

Week 0	conception – the sperm and egg join together and grow to form an embryo
Week 4	the heart begins to beat
Week 5	legs and arms begin to form
Week 6	bones begin to form
Week 9	the baby begins to look more human and is now called a fetus (or foetus)
Week 12	all organs of the body are formed
Week 14	
Week 20	eyebrows and eyelashes begin to form
Week 23	the fetus can survive outside the mother's body (with medical support)
Week 40	full term – the baby is ready to be born naturally

The development of a baby from conception to birth

DISCUSS

M

A baby girl of 21 weeks was placed in a metal dish in a back room and left to die after a hospital abortion, it was alleged last night. It was said to have taken three hours. A doctor said it was pointless trying to save the child and she was finally wrapped in a plastic bag and put into the incinerator at Carlisle's City General Hospital. One nurse who took part in the operation was so distressed that she carried out her own form of baptism.

Daily Mail, 8 February 1988

1. How do you react to Source M?
2. Do you think that such emotive descriptions are helpful in the abortion debate? Give reasons.
3. How do you think the fetus in Source M should have been disposed of?

ISSUE 2: Who should decide?

Under British law doctors can abort a baby, even after 24 weeks, **if** it is going to be severely disabled. Even when this law was being debated in 1990 critics said that it was a dangerous rule. They said that parents might ask for an abortion for minor conditions such as a cleft lip or cleft palate. The defenders of the bill just said this was scaremongering and of course doctors would not allow this to happen. But in 2002 it did happen. In a clinic in Hereford a 28-week-old fetus was aborted, at the parents' request, because the baby had a cleft lip and cleft palate. This is not the only time this has happened, but this particular case came to light because of the campaign of Joanna Jepson, Church of England curate.

What did she do?

First Joanna Jepson challenged the police to investigate. She claimed the clinic had performed an illegal abortion (a serious crime which can carry a prison sentence). The police cleared the clinic of wrongdoing. However, Jepson then took the case to the High Court. She wanted the High Court to make the law clearer. What does 'serious disability' mean? Does a cleft lip or cleft palate qualify?

O

When the law was passed it was deliberately left vague for the decision to be made between the woman and her doctors. We feel that that is appropriate. What some people will regard as extremely serious, and a condition they really feel they could not live with in a child, others would feel differently about.

Ann Furedi, chief executive of the British Pregnancy Advisory Service

N

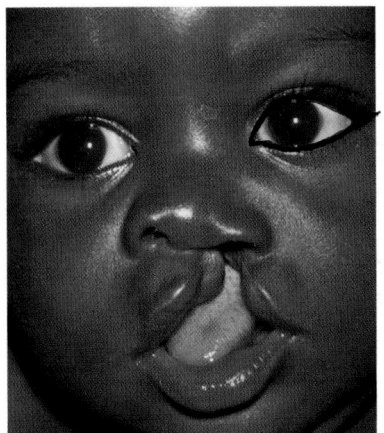 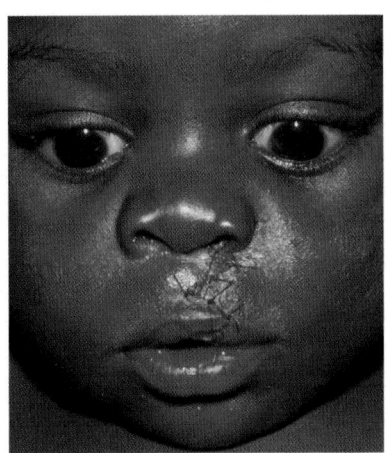

A child with a cleft lip (left); and the same child after corrective surgery

Why did she do this?

Joanna Jepson is not an absolute anti-abortionist. She can see the need for abortion in certain cases. But she believes that to treat a cleft lip or palate as a serious deformity is wrong. It can be corrected by a relatively simple operation in childhood. Children with this condition can lead perfectly normal lives. Abortion on such trivial grounds is an example of discrimination against disabled people.

She has very personal motivation: she herself was born with a serious facial deformity. Her lower jaw was out of alignment with the rest of her face. As a teenager she had surgery to correct the deformity. But she says that her suffering as a child and teenager was part of making her the person she is today.

She believes it is wrong to leave it to parents and doctors to decide what is a serious disability. Some parents, she says, might regard the absence of a finger as a serious disability. 'We need to resist the belief that the value of human life lies in physical perfection and have a wider understanding of disabilities so that disability is not seen purely in negative terms.'

DISCUSS

1 Why do you think some people regard a cleft lip and palate as a serious disability while others do not?
2 Read Source O. Why does Ann Furedi want to leave decisions like this to individual doctors and parents?
3 Why does Joanna Jepson disagree?

MINI DEBATE

Work in pairs. 'Let parents choose!' One of you has to argue for this statement and the other against it for one minute. Then swap roles and argue the other side for one minute.

SAVE AS...

Make some notes reflecting on your mini debate then go to Joanna Jepson's website – your teacher can give you the address. Write a message for the board or an e-mail that you could send her expressing your personal views on this issue.

What does it mean to die a dignified death?

Some GCSE courses put the issues of abortion and euthanasia together to compare and contrast. You can see why. Many of the key ideas that affect attitudes to abortion (particularly 'sanctity of life') are relevant here too, so keep them in mind. In this investigation you will join in the debate over voluntary euthanasia. For your final task you will write your own speech arguing for or against making euthanasia legal in Britain.

STARTER

The following is a true story which took place in the Netherlands.

The careful death of José

José was 30 years old when she asked a doctor to end her life.

She had been diabetic since childhood. The diabetes had destroyed the nerve endings in her stomach, meaning that she could not digest any food. She had to be fed through a tube which pumped liquid food directly into her intestine. Even so, liquid would seep back into her stomach and she would often vomit violently. Her weight dropped from 70 kg to 42 kg.

Her doctors tried every imaginable alternative treatment but with no effect. Finally, she asked her hospital specialist for euthanasia. He was unwilling to grant it and prescribed anti-depressant drugs instead. She took these, but they made her dull and unresponsive.

That's when her local doctor, a frequent visitor, said he was willing to consider euthanasia.

'It was a kind of relief,' said her husband Rob. 'We discussed it frequently. We both cried buckets of tears. We had a very open and honest relationship, but in the last few months the relationship went sky-high emotionally.'

Their doctor consulted a doctor appointed by the courts, and an independent doctor who gave a second opinion. A psychiatrist had to confirm José was in sound mind. Even then they had to wait four months before being 'approved' for euthanasia.

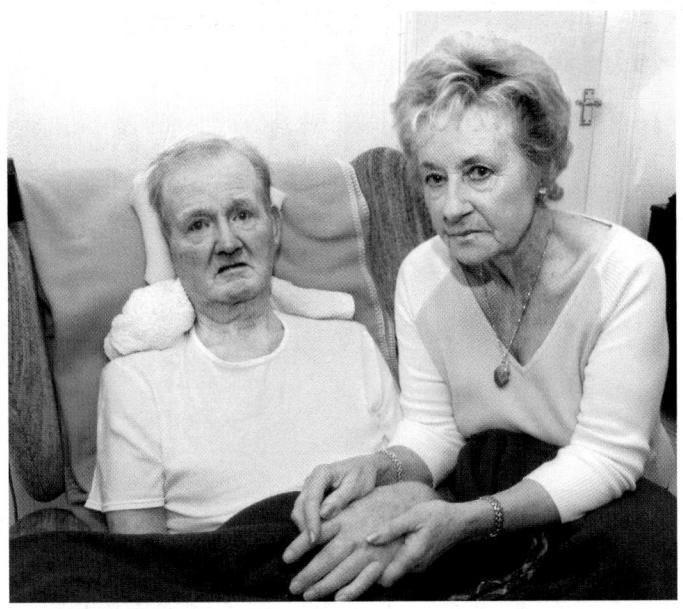

Euthanasia is also legal in other countries. Win Crew took her husband Reginald to Switzerland for euthanasia in January 2003. On her return there was a police investigation but eventually she was not charged.

DISCUSS

1 Supporters of euthanasia sometimes call it 'mercy killing'. Opponents call it 'murder'. The word actually means 'gentle and easy death'. Which term best fits the story of José?

2 Did José die a dignified death?

3 Do you find the death of José morally acceptable?

4 Do people in your class hold different opinions about José's euthanasia? If so, explain your point of view to someone who disagrees with you.

SAVE AS...

Read the Checkpoint. Use the information there to explain the correct term for José's euthanasia and whether it would be legal in Britain.

When the time came, José had planned her funeral service. The euthanasia was arranged for 8.00 p.m. on a Monday. Rob describes her last few days:

José was amazingly cool. On Saturday she had her last visit from her parents. On Monday she rang up a few people just to make sure that she had heard their voices. She dressed up the way she wanted to be cremated and did her hair. We watched a few U2 videos – her favourite band.

I asked her, 'How does it feel that you are going to die?'

She said, 'It's very restful, it's very peaceful. I can't give you the answer, but it's a good feeling. I did my trip. I fought my fight.'

Around eight o'clock she said, 'Well, I think I want a coffee because it won't come back up now!' She was on the couch with her coffee and her cigarettes when the doctors came. Our doctor said he had expected to enter a room full of emotions and sadness with family crying. He said that the obvious acceptance and serenity made it easier for him.

The doctors finally checked there were no doubts. She said, 'Well, I'm ready.'

We spent a few moments alone. What do you say? 'Have a good trip'? I had to cry. That was the strange thing – she comforted me. She said, 'It's going to be all right!'

Finally we called the doctors, and with me holding her hand she was given a narcotic to make her sleepy and then the fatal drug.

Life continues, but everybody has their own little voice and José is part of mine. She agreed to watch over me and I still think of her every day. She is there in the simple things.

✔ CHECKPOINT

What is euthanasia?
Euthanasia is the term used to describe ending a person's life deliberately, but for compassionate reasons.

Euthanasia in Britain
Euthanasia is illegal in Britain. There have been a number of attempts to get a bill through Parliament legalising euthanasia. All have failed. One example was a bill in 1969. If it had been passed, it would have allowed euthanasia on request to anyone over 18, provided that: 'two doctors believed the patient to be suffering from a serious physical illness or impairment, reasonably thought in the patient's case to be incurable, and expected to cause considerable distress.' Most recently, in 2003 the House of Lords allowed a Bill to have a second reading. Such Bills are unlikely to become law because they do not have government support.

Key terms
VOLUNTARY EUTHANASIA is when a person asks for their own life to be ended.

COMPULSORY or INVOLUNTARY EUTHANASIA is when someone else, e.g. a doctor or a family member, decides that it would be in the person's best interest to end their life.

ACTIVE EUTHANASIA is when something is done to the person to make them die more quickly, e.g. giving drugs to bring about death.

PASSIVE EUTHANASIA is when any form of treatment which might extend a person's life is taken away, e.g. turning off a life-support machine or removing a feeding tube. N.B. In Britain today this is allowed. It is not legally termed euthanasia.

ASSISTED SUICIDE means helping someone to perform their own euthanasia, for example by giving them drugs to take.

KEY CHRISTIAN BELIEFS: Euthanasia

Christians are opposed to euthanasia. Almost no Christian tradition would approve the death of José described on the previous page. Sources A–C below are examples:

Why do Christians take this strongly anti-euthanasia view? There is nothing specific in the Bible about it. Instead they refer back to basic principles.

ACTIVITY

1 Which of these principles are being used in Sources A and B?
2 What other argument is being used in Source C? Add it to the fourth weight in your own copy of this diagram.
3 Christians believe there is a life after death. On which side of the scales would you put this belief and why?

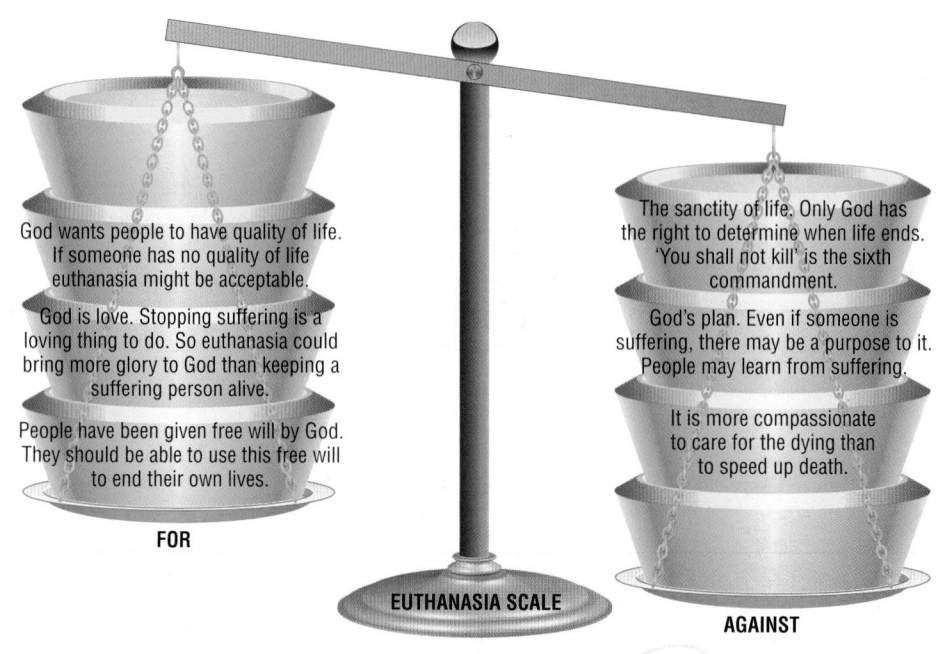

FOR

God wants people to have quality of life. If someone has no quality of life euthanasia might be acceptable.

God is love. Stopping suffering is a loving thing to do. So euthanasia could bring more glory to God than keeping a suffering person alive.

People have been given free will by God. They should be able to use this free will to end their own lives.

EUTHANASIA SCALE

AGAINST

The sanctity of life. Only God has the right to determine when life ends. 'You shall not kill' is the sixth commandment.

God's plan. Even if someone is suffering, there may be a purpose to it. People may learn from suffering.

It is more compassionate to care for the dying than to speed up death.

 ## CHECKPOINT

What about passive euthanasia?
Christians are almost all opposed to voluntary euthanasia. However Christians do disagree about passive euthanasia, for example, turning off a life-support machine or prescribing pain killing drugs which also, as a side effect, hasten death. Even the Catholic tradition which holds such a strong pro-life stance allows doctors to prescribe pain-killing drugs even if they might have the side effect of shortening life. And most Christians agree that where a person is being kept alive simply by a life-support machine, it is morally acceptable to turn off that machine if the relatives wish it since the person's natural life has already ended. It is only the inventions of modern technology that are making life possible in this case.

A

No one has the right to bring about death by their own decision, whether by suicide or by voluntary euthanasia. Christians through the ages have found that the grace of God sustains heart and mind to the end in difficult situations and so can Christians today who face painful or drawn-out death.

Salvation Army guidance on euthanasia

B

The Catholic Church believes that euthanasia is wrong. Life is sacred. Only God can make decisions over death. The Pope said euthanasia was contributing to a 'profound change in the way life and relationships between people are considered' and called it 'a grave violation of the Law of God' (Encyclical, March 1995). Cardinal Basil Hume, Archbishop of Westminster, said he was '200 per cent' behind the Pope's teaching on this. He said in The Times, *31 March 1995, 'My plea is that society should stop and ask, where could all this lead?'*

A summary of Catholic teaching on euthanasia

C

The pleas of gravely ill people who sometimes ask for death are not to be understood as implying a true desire for euthanasia; in fact, it is almost always a case of an anguished plea for help and love. What a sick person needs, besides medical care, is love, the human and supernatural warmth with which the sick person can and ought to be surrounded by all those close to him or her, parents and children, doctors and nurses.

Catholic declaration on euthanasia, 5 May 1980

KEY CHRISTIAN BELIEFS: Quality of life?

One of the most important ideas that comes up in discussions about euthanasia is 'quality of life'. People say that someone with no quality of life should be allowed to die. This is particularly relevant to discussions about passive euthanasia. Let's look at this in more detail.

How people judge quality of life

1 Look at Sources D and E. Who do you think has the best quality of life? Give reasons.

2 Now imagine that the woman in Source D has got an incurable disease which means she cannot move herself. She has been helped to the swimming pool by a servant who has put the drink in her hand for her to suck through a straw. Does this affect your answer to Question 1?

3 Now imagine the woman in Source E is about to be evicted from her flat. She has no home to go to. No family. No money. No friends. The woman in Source D has a loving family who come to visit her every day to keep her company. She can talk to them even though she cannot move. Does this affect your previous answer?

4 Invent some more information about either person that you think would affect their quality of life for better or worse.

D

E

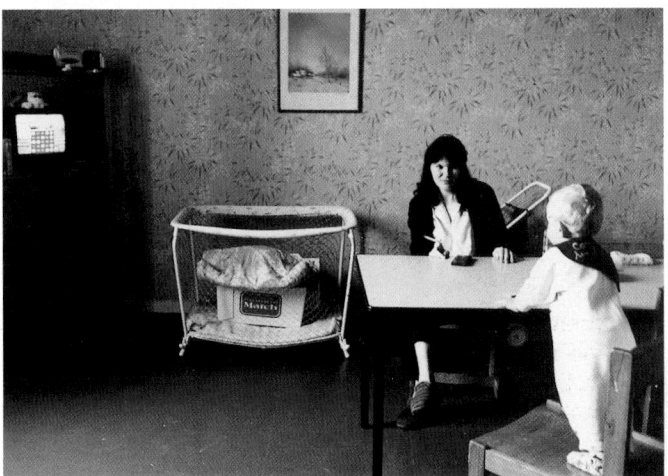

ACTIVITY

1 Finish this sentence in as many different ways as you wish: 'Quality of life is ...'

2 Tick any statements which Christians might agree with.

3 Put a cross by any statements which Christians would reject.

SAVE AS

4 Write a paragraph explaining how the idea of quality of life is relevant to decisions about:
a) euthanasia
b) abortion.

How the Bible judges quality of life

Christians believe that God wants people to live a fulfilled life. One of Jesus' most famous sayings, often quoted in this context, is 'I have come that you might have life in all its fullness' (John 10.10). From the rest of Jesus' teaching it is clear that he thought someone's quality of life was determined not by their possessions but by

❑ their relationship with God
❑ their relationship with others
❑ their feeling of rightness in themselves.

You cannot therefore see quality of life. You cannot even judge someone else's quality of life. It also follows that quality of life does not mean a pain-free life. Even someone in great pain who is terminally ill and has no hope of recovery might still have a reasonable quality of life because quality of life is about inner life. Even if someone does feel they have poor quality of life the Christian response is not to end their life but to do all they can to try to improve it. Over the page we investigate this in more detail.

CASE STUDY: The hospice movement – A Christian alternative to euthanasia

ACTIVITY

The sources and information on this page tell you about the origins, the motivation and the achievements of the hospice movement.

Work in groups. Prepare a leaflet or a PowerPoint presentation about the work of the hospice movement. Your leaflet or presentation should be targeted at Christian churches and should aim to raise money and/or volunteers.

You will need to read through the sources and consider what points to use in your leaflet or presentation. You should include at least:

a) an explanation of what a hospice is – and what it aims to achieve

b) a quote from someone who works in a hospice

c) a summary of how someone who gives money or volunteer time to a hospice might be helping the terminally ill.

What is a hospice?

A hospice looks after people who are terminally ill. They are cared for by a wide range of trained medical staff supported by volunteers. Their pain is relieved through drugs. Any fears about death that they or their families may have are talked about.

The first hospices were founded by Christians who were at the forefront in looking for compassionate alternatives to euthanasia. The hospice movement has now spread worldwide.

Cicely Saunders and the start of the hospice movement

Cicely Saunders became a Christian while at Oxford University in the 1940s. Against the advice of friends and family, she became a nurse. The turning point in her career was when she worked on a cancer ward in a London hospital. She was troubled by the way doctors ignored the needs of patients who were terminally ill. She watched many of them die virtually alone.

She approached the hospital managers with an idea she had to surround those dying of cancer with friends and loved ones during their last days, rather than isolating them in sterile rooms with strangers. Her radical ideas were rejected. So she decided to become a doctor herself and make them happen. She enrolled in medical school. Six years later at the age of 39 she graduated and began her work to develop and spread the hospice idea – caring for the dying, motivated by Christian compassion.

The first hospice opened was St Christopher's in south-east London in 1967. Since then the movement has spread around the world.

I'm against euthanasia for a positive reason; I have seen people achieve so much in the ending of their lives – times that their families would have missed. It's often time after they might have asked to opt out when they perhaps would have gone in bitterness, whereas they finally go in peace and fulfilment.

Dame Cicely Saunders, a Christian doctor and founder of the hospice movement

Focus on St Christopher's

A volunteer talks with a resident in St. Christopher's chapel.

St Christopher's Hospice is:

- *a Christian foundation with staff and volunteers of many denominations or none*
- *a medical foundation, working to improve the quality of life remaining for people [with terminal illnesses]*
- *open to all who need its care, regardless of race, creed or ability to pay*
- *researching the support needed by dying patients and their families, in the hospice and at home*
- *a charity, built entirely with gifts and grants … funded by the generosity of friends and supporters.*

From an annual report of St Christopher's Hospice, South London, founded by Cicely Saunders in the 1960s

Hospice volunteer David Stone explains how he started as a volunteer

I am so glad my mother came here to die. In the hospice she was cared for as a whole person, and my family and I were helped to deal with losing her. She had lived a long and happy life and I was very concerned that she should not leave this life in pain. The doctors and nurses helped her to manage her pain, and the Catholic priest was always there for us. My mother died peacefully in my arms with her family around her. That time in the hospice gave us the time to prepare for death and to tell her that we loved her. I had never been to a hospice before my mother went in, but now I work as a volunteer there to help and support other families.

In Korea, a group of Christians are caring for terminally ill patients who have nowhere else to go

In the peaceful environment of Saemmul, patients spend their last days restfully, while still receiving the care they need. Thanks to donations, the hospice provides its services free. Its assistants serve on a voluntary basis.

They work tirelessly to ensure a germ-free environment, and they help patients with basic tasks like eating, dressing, and getting cleaned up. But hospice workers also have a deeper concern – they care about their patients' spiritual condition. Twice a day, workers take patients to worship services led by Pastor Won Ju-Hee who is also Director of Saemmul Hospice. "Love starts from taking an interest in others," he said. "When we call each person's name in prayer, we express love and share their pain." The hospice workers also assist Pastor Won in bedside baptism services for patients who want them. This ceremony helps hospice residents deal with death as a spiritual as well as a physical reality.

Pastor Won said 'Leading one person to heaven at the end of his or her life, and completing the life of that person as a beautiful life, helps the patient and his or her family, as well as being a great honour for us."

With workers who have a heart to serve, typical of Christians, Saemmul Hospice has become a special kind of ministry. Patients here can find hope with God, and live out the rest of their days knowing that even when they die, they will die with dignity. Hospices were first introduced to Korea in 1991. Now, some 1,500 volunteers care for hospice patients free of charge. These volunteers often begin by caring for their own family members, then stay on to care for others.

From a news report for CWN by Deborah Lim, 15 August 2003

Rev Ronald C Purkey explains his Christian motivation in setting up and running Hope Hospice in Indiana, USA, which started on 14 April 1995.

Our motivation is to bring comfort and care to terminally ill patients and their families. We seek staff members and volunteers with a Christian philosophy of life. We seek helpers who want to give comfort, love and care.

We use medication to deal with pain, and we give emotional and spiritual support to the patient and the patient's family. We pray with them. We read the Bible to them. We show them love. And we try to give them hope.

My wife and I have been blessed by helping others who are suffering. I have been a minister for over 40 years. My wife, Sarah, has been a nurse for nearly 45 years. We started Hope Hospice as a Christian ministry – as a way for Sarah and me to serve the Lord Jesus Christ. Hope Hospice has been one of the biggest blessings in our life together. It is wonderful to be able to help others during their time of need.

ISSUE: Should voluntary euthanasia be allowed in Britain?

F

In every case, care is more merciful than killing.

The fatal tide of permissiveness is trying to persuade us that euthanasia – so clearly condemned as a criminal act and for centuries specially spurned in the Hippocratic oath – may now be acceptable, or even caring. Having spent two decades looking after patients dying in my general practice, I must disdain it as fundamentally wrong, entirely unnecessary when good practice takes place, and so widely open to abuse that it must continue to be highly unethical and illegal.

The strongest argument against euthanasia – apart from the moral one – is that there has never been greater ability to relieve pain and never more people professing to care for and cherish those in need. In our wealthy society there should be no need for termination of the sick.

A. Rogers, a Christian doctor, writing in the *Independent*, 12 May 1990

Euthanasia is illegal in Britain, but the Voluntary Euthanasia Society campaigns for the law to be changed to allow it within a strictly controlled legal framework as in the Netherlands, where euthanasia remains illegal, but provided certain procedures are carefully followed, a doctor who administers euthanasia will not be prosecuted in the courts. The Voluntary Euthanasia Society have campaigned on behalf of individuals such as Diane Pretty, who want euthanasia, arguing it is their right under the Human Rights Act.

G

Diane Pretty and her husband arrive at the high court in 2001 for a judicial review into her voluntary euthanasia. She was 43, mentally alert, but motor neurone disease had left her unable to move independently and unable to talk. She wanted the court to guarantee they would not prosecute her husband Brian if he helped her to die. You can read about the case at www.justice4diane.org.uk. Diane died in 2002.

Most proposals for euthanasia give the key role to doctors. What do they think? Sources F and I give two viewpoints. In a recent confidential survey 18 per cent of Catholic doctors in the USA said they would administer euthanasia if requested by a terminally ill patient. In another survey one in eight Australian doctors admitted that they had helped someone to die at their request. British doctors have also admitted to helping the terminally ill to die. In the vast majority of cases doctors say they shortened the life of a terminally ill and suffering patient by only a matter of days. Doctors who have performed euthanasia are totally convinced they are helping the person not harming them.

H

We have 20,000 requests for 'living wills' each year, showing that a large proportion of the British people would like to see voluntary euthanasia become legal. Using euthanasia would save scarce medical resources which could then be used to help those who can be cured, they say. Everyone should be able to have 'the mercy of a painless death'.

Comment from a member of the Voluntary Euthanasia Society. In a living will a person asks for euthanasia in the event that they become terminally ill and unable to communicate their own decision to relatives or doctors.

I

My patients can be sure that I will not let them suffer unnecessarily alone. That is my goal and my duty as a doctor.

Having the option of euthanasia makes it possible to concentrate not on the anxieties of suffering but on what people really want to do before they are going to die – like reconciliation with family members, saying their goodbyes, making a last trip downtown or out of the country. It really takes care of the burden of potential suffering which hovers over their heads like a shadow.

Euthanasia is not just about ending someone's life, but about how a life ends.

Doctor Gerrit Kimsma, a Dutch doctor and teacher of medical ethics who has performed euthanasia six times.

FOCUS TASK

You are going to have a class debate on the motion: 'This house believes that voluntary euthanasia should be allowed in Britain.'

Stage 1 Preparing
To help you prepare for the debate:

1 Study all these quotations. Some of them are simply reminders of arguments from earlier pages. Others are new ideas.
2 Divide them into arguments for and arguments against the motion.
3 Add any other arguments from earlier pages that you think should also be included for and against.
4 Highlight in one colour any of the arguments that you particularly agree with. Put a note alongside it saying why you think this is a strong argument.

> It's a free world. If someone wants euthanasia, who has the right to say no? It's up to them.

> Anyone who knows about Nazi Germany could never support euthanasia. One thing leads to another. Euthanasia was the thin end of the wedge. The Nazis started by killing the mentally ill. They ended up slaughtering Jews by the millions.

> Euthanasia is happening already – for example, people travel to other countries, where it is legal, to die. We should bring British law into line with other countries where it is allowed.

> Euthanasia is putting someone to sleep lovingly. Euthanasia can be an act of love. Love cannot be illegal.

> It is impossible to make any euthanasia law that would work in all cases. It would be a nightmare. It all depends on the circumstances.

> What marks out humans from animals – you could call it our God-given ability – is that we have minds to think and reason things out. We should not be scared of using our minds to decide if it is right to allow someone to die. Let's have a law which gives intelligent people responsibility for approving any request to die.

> The most caring and loving thing to do is to care for someone who wants to die, to give them love and give them hope.

> People change their minds. What if I write my living will, then after I'm too ill to talk or communicate, I regret it? Imagine someone coming to 'turn you off' and you can do nothing about it. No way.

5 Highlight in another colour any arguments that you think are particularly weak. Put a note alongside saying why you think they are particularly weak.

Stage 2 Writing your speech
A good speech for a debate has four parts.

- A clear introduction stating whether you are for or against the motion
- Your main reason for your view. Focus on one reason – your strongest one. Include any evidence to support it.
- An attack on any opposition arguments that are weak. Again focus on just one.
- A conclusion calling on people to support your view when it comes to the vote and a reminder of the main reason they should do so.

Your teacher can give you a planning sheet to help you write your speech.

ACTIVITY

Work in pairs. Either:

1 Dr Gerrit Kimsma (Source I) meets Dr A. Rogers (Source F). Role-play a conversation in which they discuss euthanasia.

Or:

2 All doctors take the Hippocratic oath when they qualify. In this oath they swear to 'do everything possible to preserve and restore life and not to take it.' Discuss whether this oath should be changed today. Give reasons for your answer.

3.1

Are Christian ideas about marriage out of date?

Christians believe that the quality of human relationships matter to God. The Bible is full of advice on what makes a good relationship and Christian principles on sex, marriage and divorce have provided the blueprint for society in the past. However popular attitudes are changing. Should Christians change as well or should they hold firm to traditional principles? See what you think as you investigate Christian attitudes to sex, marriage, divorce and family life. For your final task you will prepare a leaflet summarising Christian ideas about personal relationships. What will you emphasise: old ideas or new?

ACTIVITY

Find out where you stand on the attitude scale with our Quick Quiz.

1 On your own, try this quiz. Choose the answers that are closest to your own views. Be honest. Note down your answers on a separate sheet of paper.

2 When you have finished, work out with your teacher where you are on the attitude scale.

3 Compare your results with those of the rest of the class. Do you think your class is typical?

Are you the marrying kind?

1. Could you survive happily without a steady boyfriend or girlfriend for a few months?
   a) No! I'll go out with anyone to avoid being single.
   b) Yes! I don't want to rush into any old relationship.
   c) Definitely! I'm waiting for the perfect partner.
   d) Yes! I prefer being free.

2. How would you feel if, in the future, your parents tried to influence your choice of marriage partner?
   a) I'd be very cross! It's none of their business who I marry.
   b) I wouldn't like to be pushed into something, but I would not rule out doing what they want.
   c) I'd be horrified. What a thought!
   d) I'd welcome their support. They know best.

3. Do you think it's OK to have sex before marriage?
   a) Yes! It builds up a relationship.
   b) No! I'd like to be a virgin when I get married.

   c) Definitely! I'm not going to get sex any other way.
   d) Maybe, but only if I intended to marry the person anyway.

4. Would you like to spend the whole of your life married to the same person?
   a) I can't imagine that at all. Boring!
   b) Nice idea, if it works.
   c) Of course! That's the whole point of marriage.
   d) I'd like it! If I manage to choose the right person in the first place.

5. Do you think that children are better off if their parents are married?
   a) Yes, absolutely! You shouldn't have children without marriage.
   b) It's more important for parents to be loving than to be married.
   c) Yes! I feel a happy marriage provides the best environment for children.
   d) No! Why should they be?

6. If you got married, would you have a religious ceremony?
   a) Definitely! I want a big white wedding in a church.

   b) I'd like a religious ceremony, but I can do without all the extras like presents and banquets.
   c) Some kind of ceremony, but not a religious one!
   d) I don't want any sort of wedding, religious or otherwise.

7. If you were married, how do you think you would react if your partner had an affair with someone else?
   a) I'd cope! These things happen, don't they?
   b) I'd be upset, but I'd work hard to rebuild the relationship.
   c) Shattered! I'd want a divorce immediately.
   d) I'd probably go off and do the same myself.

✅ CHECKPOINT

Popular attitudes to sex, marriage and divorce are changing in Britain. Today:

- Seventy-five per cent of couples live together before marriage
- Forty-one per cent of marriages end in divorce – an all-time high
- Britain has one of the highest divorce rates in Europe
- Fewer than half the weddings in Britain take place in a church.

Despite these statistics, it is still the aim of the overwhelming majority of people in Britain to get married. And in a recent survey, 84 per cent of all women and 79 per cent of all men thought adultery was wrong.

⭐ KEY CHRISTIAN BELIEFS: Marriage is . . .

There is widespread agreement among Christians about the nature and purpose of a Christian marriage. This example comes from the Catholic Truth Society.

8. If you get married who will be the boss in your relationship?
   a) Husband in charge; wife to obey.
   b) Me! I love getting my own way.
   c) We'd be equals – you don't need anyone 'in charge' of a relationship.
   d) But I told you – I don't want to get married!

9. Your boyfriend/girlfriend suggests you get married. You are in love but you aren't sure you want to spend your lives together. What do you do?
   a) I'd say yes! We can always get divorced if it doesn't work out.
   b) I'd say no! I've got to be 100% certain. Divorce would be a disaster.
   c) I'd say maybe! Then talk over my fears with my partner.
   d) I don't want to get married.

A sacrament is a religious ritual by which Christians can know God better.

Marriage unites two Christian people before God.

Marriage is for life.

Love and sex are important parts of the partnership.

Wife and husband help and support one another. The marriage relationship is as much about giving as taking.

A

*Marriage is the **sacrament** in which a **baptised** man and woman vow to belong to each other in a **permanent**, exclusive, **sexual** partnership of loving, mutual care, concern and **shared** responsibility in the hope of having **children** and bringing up a **family**.*

People should have only one wife or husband. This is known as monogamy. Sex outside marriage (adultery) is not permitted. 'Do not commit adultery' is the seventh of the Ten Commandments.

The couple are expected to have children.

Family life is the basis for society.

SAVE AS ...

Here are four important words from Source A:

- belong
- partnership
- mutual
- shared.

They all have similar meanings. Check the meanings in a dictionary if you need to then write one sentence to summarise what these words have in common and what that tells you about the Christian view of marriage.

KEY CHRISTIAN BELIEFS: Sex

The Bible offers two distinct messages about sex.

Sex is to be celebrated ...

According to the Bible, God's very first instruction to Adam and Eve was to go and have sex. The Bible says that when Creation was finished God thought everything – including sex – was very good! Sex is a pleasure, a gift and a joy. It is one of the things that holds a relationship together. One of the most under-used books of the Bible is King Solomon's poem celebrating love and sex, *The Song of Songs*, also called *The Song of Solomon* (see Source B).

B

THE SONG OF SONGS

His eyes, too, are doves
                    dipping in clear water
yet as if they had splashed in milk.
His cheeks are smooth couches
                        scenting of spices.
His lips are red anemone-colour
moist with the breath of myrrh.
His arms are subtle as gold
                    round
and studded with great jewels of Tarshish.
His rod is arrogant ivory
                     flushed with sapphire-blue;
and his thighs are marble columns
                      in sockets of pure gold.
Erect
       he looks like Lebanon
                  a king among cedars.
But when he speaks it is soft and sweet.

  I love him
           whole and entire I love him.
This is my Beloved,
              women of Jerusalem,
Oh women.

Engraving and extract from a poetic adaptation of *The Song of Solomon* published by the Ark Press

But sex is also to be controlled

Christianity teaches that sex belongs within marriage. Chastity (abstaining from sex before marriage) and fidelity (not having sex with anyone else once you are married) are valued very highly. 'Do not commit adultery' is one of the Ten Commandments. A common theme in the writing of St Paul in the New Testament is that Christians should not follow the sexual morality of the society around them but should aim for sexual restraint and control. For example, in writing to the Christians in the Greek city of Corinth – where promiscuity (casual sex) and prostitution were common – he said:

C

You know that your bodies are parts of the body of Christ. Shall I take a part of Christ's body and make it part of the body of a prostitute? Impossible! ...

Avoid immorality. Any other sin a man commits does not affect his body; but the man who is guilty of sexual immorality sins against his own body. Don't you know that your body is the temple of the Holy Spirit, who lives in you?

1 Corinthians 6.15–19

DISCUSS

Compare Sources B and C. Both are from the Bible. Is there any contradiction between them? Explain your answer.

⦿ ISSUE: Why do many Christians keep sex for marriage?

The negative 'control' message has been sounded rather more loudly by Christians in the past than the positive 'joy of sex' message. Sometimes this was for the purely practical reason that chastity has always been the surest method of contraception – for many centuries it was the only reliable method. However, many Christians would say that there are positive rather than negative reasons to keep sex for marriage (see Source D).

D

makes it part of a **legal contract**

balances the joy of sex with **responsibility** to the other person

Keeping sex within marriage gives it a special status...

makes it dependent on a **commitment** to spend the rest of your life with someone

makes it part of a **religious** or **spiritual covenant**

E

A demonstration outside the US congress building by supporters of the 'True Love Waits' movement

F

True Love Waits

Believing that true love waits, I make a commitment to god, myself, my family, those I date, my future mate and my future children to be sexually pure until the day I enter a covenant marriage relationship.

Jim Christensen

A pledge card held by a 15-year-old member of the 'True Love Waits' movement, which began in Nashville, USA, in 1992. In a special ceremony, Christian children make a promise not to have sex before marriage. Parents give a ring to the child, saying 'let this ring be a constant reminder to you to be sexually pure'.

DISCUSS

1 Read Source F. Do you think it is right for Christian parents to influence their children in their sexual lives? If so, at what age do you think it would be appropriate to use this ceremony?

SAVE AS ...

2 Make your own copy of Diagram D, explaining it in your own words.

ISSUE: Should the Catholic Church change its teaching on contraception?

CHECKPOINT

Types of contraception
A contraceptive is anything designed to stop sex leading to conception. **Artificial** contraceptives include drugs such as the pill and physical barriers such as the condom. A **natural** method of contraception is the rhythm method.

Family planning means using contraception to plan when to have children.

Christian teaching on contraception
For many centuries the Christian Churches were opposed to any form of contraception. Most Protestant Churches now see responsible use of contraception within marriage as entirely acceptable. They argue it benefits a relationship as it allows sex to be enjoyed without the fear of unwanted pregnancy and it ensures that any children are wanted.

However, the Catholic Church has continued to oppose all forms of contraception other than the rhythm method. The four main reasons are:

- **The sanctity of life**: (see page 14).
- **God makes the decisions**: It is up to God to decide how many children a couple should have; contraception interferes with God's plan.
- **The purpose of sex**: God wants people to multiply and populate the Earth. God has given sex for the purpose of having children, so all acts of sex should allow for this.
- **Sex should not be devalued**: Reliable contraceptives encourage people to have casual sex with many partners. This is against God's law which is for people to only have sex within marriage.

The Catholic church is against contraception (see Checkpoint). This traditional teaching is being challenged by various modern developments.

1 The population explosion

In the past, infant mortality was so high that mothers had to have many children in order for some to survive. Now, improving health care around the world has led to many more children surviving and the world population growing much more quickly than ever before. Population growth is fastest in poorer countries which sometimes makes the problem of poverty even worse. Reliable contraception can help raise the standard of living, education and health in a family and in society at large as there are fewer children to care for. How can the Catholic Church – the largest denomination in the world – continue to forbid Catholics from using contraception to limit the size of their families?

2 Women's rights

Most people now accept that women have equal rights to men. One part of this is to be able to control whether they have children. Reliable contraception also improves women's health. How can the Church forbid women something which enhances their life opportunities and improves their health?

3 HIV/AIDS

G

The world is in the grip of an extreme AIDS epidemic. Far from slowing down, this epidemic is speeding up. Almost 3 million people died of AIDS in 2003 and the number is increasing. Four new people are being infected every minute. The deaths wreck families. The impact on the worst hit countries is unimaginable; teachers and doctors die, businesses are ruined, the workforce is decimated. The vast majority of these new victims are infected through unprotected sex. How can the Church, which preaches the sanctity of life, forbid people from using condoms which might well save their life? Some Catholics believe that they can't!

Poster from the Catholic campaigning organisation condoms4life.org

Case study: The debate in Southern Africa

Sub-Saharan Africa is particularly damaged by the AIDS epidemic. In some areas, up to 70 per cent of the adult population is HIV positive.

Health experts are all agreed that using condoms can help prevent the transmission of AIDS. Some public health campaigners, including Christians, have urged people to use condoms if they are having sex unless they are absolutely sure that neither they nor their partner is HIV positive. Others, often Catholic Christians, have rejected this view; they argue the best response to the spread of sexually transmitted diseases, including HIV, is faithfulness to one partner and restraint from sexual intercourse outside marriage.

H

Young people need the virtues of abstinence, self-control, postponement of pleasure and sometimes if we allow ourselves to agree that all that stands between life and death of a whole people is only a piece of rubber, meaning a condom, then we are doomed already.

Janet Museveni, quoting her husband, the president of Uganda

J

It is sad that one of the few methods of preventing the transmission of HIV, and thus saving the lives of millions of our people, has been characterised as immoral and misguided.

South Africa's Health Department, July 2001

K

If we simply proclaim a message that condoms cannot be used under any circumstances, either directly or through not trying to articulate a proper response to the crisis we face, then I believe people will find difficulty in believing that we are committed as a Church to a compassionate and caring response to people who are suffering, often in appalling living conditions.

Bishop Kevin Dowling of Rustenburg, South Africa

I

Bishops reject condoms in battle against AIDS

Condoms are an 'immoral and misguided weapon' in the fight against AIDS and could be one of the main reasons for the spread of the disease, the Catholic Church in southern Africa has proclaimed. According to a statement released by a conference of bishops from South Africa, Botswana and Swaziland, the use of condoms fuels the HIV epidemic by contributing to 'the breaking down of self-control and mutual respect'. Married couples can use condoms when one or both of them is HIV-positive, provided they abstain from sex while the woman is ovulating. In this way there would be no artificial barrier to the propagation of life. It concludes: 'Abstain and be faithful is the human and Christian way of overcoming HIV/AIDS'.

The Southern African Bishops' Conference, 2001

Bishop Dowling said he had been moved to question the status quo by his own personal experience of the AIDS epidemic in his diocese. The mining region is one of the hot-spots in a country in which up to five million people, or more than one in ten, now carry the HIV virus. Bishop Dowling believes the Church could approve condoms for 'preventing the transmission of death, and therefore not as a contraceptive to prevent the transmission of life'. His views are believed to have the tacit support of many priests and nuns dealing with HIV/AIDS in communities, and received editorial backing from the main Catholic newspaper in South Africa, the *Southern Cross*.

ACTIVITY

1 Copy and complete this table.

Source	Person	For or against condoms	Why?	Your evaluation
H				
I				
J				
K				

2 'Condoms should not be used under any circumstances.' Do you agree?

This is an evaluation style question. This type of question will be very important in your exam. For this one you need to consider:

a) Why do many Catholic Christians hold this view?

b) Why do others disagree?

c) What is your own viewpoint?

This makes sure you will:

- summarise the different arguments given, to show that you understand the issues of disagreement
- state your own point of view on the issue, giving reasons for your answer.

Your teacher can also give you a sheet to help you.

★ KEY CHRISTIAN BELIEFS: Marriage

✓ CHECKPOINT

Some traditions see marriage as a SACRAMENT – something made by God which cannot be dissolved. Others see it as a contract or COVENANT. A contract is an agreement between two people to do (or not to do) something. A covenant means the same – but usually carries with it the idea that the contract is drawn up in the sight of God.

Christian marriage usually begins with a church wedding. Each tradition has its own ceremonies, but Source L shows some common features.

L

> I give you this ring as a sign of our marriage. With my body I honour you, all that I am I give to you, and all that I have I share with you … within the love of God, Father, Son and Holy Spirit.

Order of Service

1. Hymn — to focus everyone's minds on God
2. Opening statement — summarises what marriage is for (see Source N opposite)
3. Declaration — the witnesses and the couple are asked if there is any reason the couple cannot get married
4. Promises or vows — the couple make their promises to God and to one another in the presence of witnesses (see Source O)
5. Exchange of rings
6. Proclamation — the couple are now husband and wife
7. Prayers for the couple — and often a talk or a sermon about marriage
8. The register is signed by the couple and witnesses — to record that the marriage is legal
9. Closing worship — followed by photos and a reception or party

DISCUSS

1. A church wedding has many different elements. Discuss with a partner what is happening in the photographs in Source M.
   a) What part of the service does each photograph show?
   b) What is the significance of each part?
2. Many people who do not attend church still want to get married in church. Why do you think this is?
3. Should a minister or priest be prepared to marry non-churchgoers in a church? Give your reasons.

SAVE AS …

4. Each part of the marriage service is included for a reason. Some are legal, some are social and some are religious. Choose what you think are the four most important features from Source L. Explain why they are included and whether their purpose is legal, social or religious.

M

The marriage journey

A wedding is a beginning, not an end. The real point is what follows. The wedding should set you off in the right direction for a marriage journey. Let's look at the words that are said and the promises that are made at the marriage service about that journey.

N

1

I was very reluctant to get married, for all sorts of reasons, but I am really glad we did. My partner insisted our relationship be blessed by God, it was very important to him – so we had a proper church wedding. Once I had got through the stress of preparing for it I was able to share his joy. The service itself was wonderful; a huge candle-lit church and in the company of all our friends. It has really set us up for a very happy marriage.

We planned the service together. Sometimes we kept to tradition and at other times developed our own distinctive ideas. One friend sang part of the Song of Solomon *set to music. Other friends read from the Bible. Four people made short speeches about us and their beliefs about marriage and two friends wrote special prayers.*

2

By marrying we have been able to create a new family, beginning with ourselves and growing as we had our two children. We see marriage as the ideal basis for family life. We feel our children will learn what committed, loving relationships are all about through their experience of the commitment between their mother and father.

But marriage is not just for the benefit of children. There is a deep desire within us all for someone with whom we can be totally open and honest emotionally, spiritually and physically. We share God's love. Our marriage gives us a chance to grow into all that God has for us both.

Two of this book's authors reflect on their own experiences of marriage

... marriage is a gift of God in creation ... a holy mystery in which man and woman become one flesh. It is God's purpose that husband and wife shall be united in love as Christ is united with his Church.

Marriage is given,

that a husband and wife may comfort and help each other, living faithfully together in need and in plenty, in sorrow and in joy ...

that with delight and tenderness they may know each other in love, and, through the joy of their bodily union, may strengthen the union of their hearts and lives ...

that they may have children and be blessed in caring for them and bringing them up in accordance with God's will, to his praise and glory.

In marriage husband and wife belong to one another, and they begin a new life together in the community. It is a way of life that all should honour; and it must not be undertaken carelessly, lightly or selfishly, but reverently, responsibly, and after serious thought ...

we pray with them, that, strengthened and guided by God, they may fulfil his purpose for the whole of their earthly life together.

Abridged from the Anglican marriage service in *The Alternative Service Book*, 1980

P

I take you to be my husband/wife, To have and to hold from this day forward, For better, for worse, For richer, for poorer, In sickness and in health, To love and to cherish till death us do part, According to God's holy law. And to this I pledge myself.

A vow like this is used in most Christian marriage services.

The different Christian traditions agree strongly about marriage. Because marriage is a major, life-long commitment, Churches prepare couples carefully for it. Marriage courses are common. Church leaders will counsel and pray with couples and discuss Christian teaching about marriage.

ACTIVITY

1 Read Sources O and P. Draw up two lists:
   a) what is expected of the married couple;
   b) qualities that the couple will need to meet these expectations.

DISCUSS

2 Elaine Storkey, an evangelical writer, has said, 'Despite expensive weddings, every marriage in the West gets off to a bad start because we have to unlearn individualism and learn community.' What do you think she means? Do you agree with her? Refer to your lists from question 1 and also refer to Source N.

SAVE AS ...

3 Write Five Golden Rules for a Christian marriage. Put a star by the most important one(s).

Married to God?

Not everyone wants to get married. Others want to, but never meet the right partner. A small number of Christians decide not to marry because they want to devote their life to God instead. Some traditions, such as the Catholic Church, reserve a high place for those such as priests, monks or nuns who take this vow of celibacy.

KEY CHRISTIAN BELIEFS: Family life

SAVE AS …

The diagram below does not show all the pressures or all the supports. On your own copy of the diagram, add other examples you can think of.

All Christian traditions put a high value on family life. In some cultures the typical family is a 'nuclear family' (parents and children). In others, it is an 'extended family', which also includes grandparents and other relatives. In either case, the family is seen as part of God's plan for caring for individuals. In the Christian family young children are nurtured; the old are respected and cared for; religious and moral values are learned; young people are moulded into mature adults.

In most Christian traditions, parents also promise to raise their children as Christians, although how Christian parents do this varies greatly.

In the Bible, the fifth of the Ten Commandments is, 'Respect your father and mother.' This is reinforced in the New Testament, for example in Ephesians 6.1–4, where the writer says: 'Children: it is your Christian duty to obey your parents … so that all may go well with you.' Equally, parents also have a duty to: 'not treat your children in a way to make them angry. Instead bring them up with Christian discipline and instruction.'

The Church family

Christians refer to the Church as being like a family. Some refer to other Christians as their brothers and sisters. God is seen as a parent. Jesus taught his disciples to pray to 'our Father'. Many of the values that Christians apply to family life have their equivalent in the Church – the young are nurtured, the old are cared for.

As society develops, the changes put pressure on family life. How does the church respond? Source Q summarises.

Q

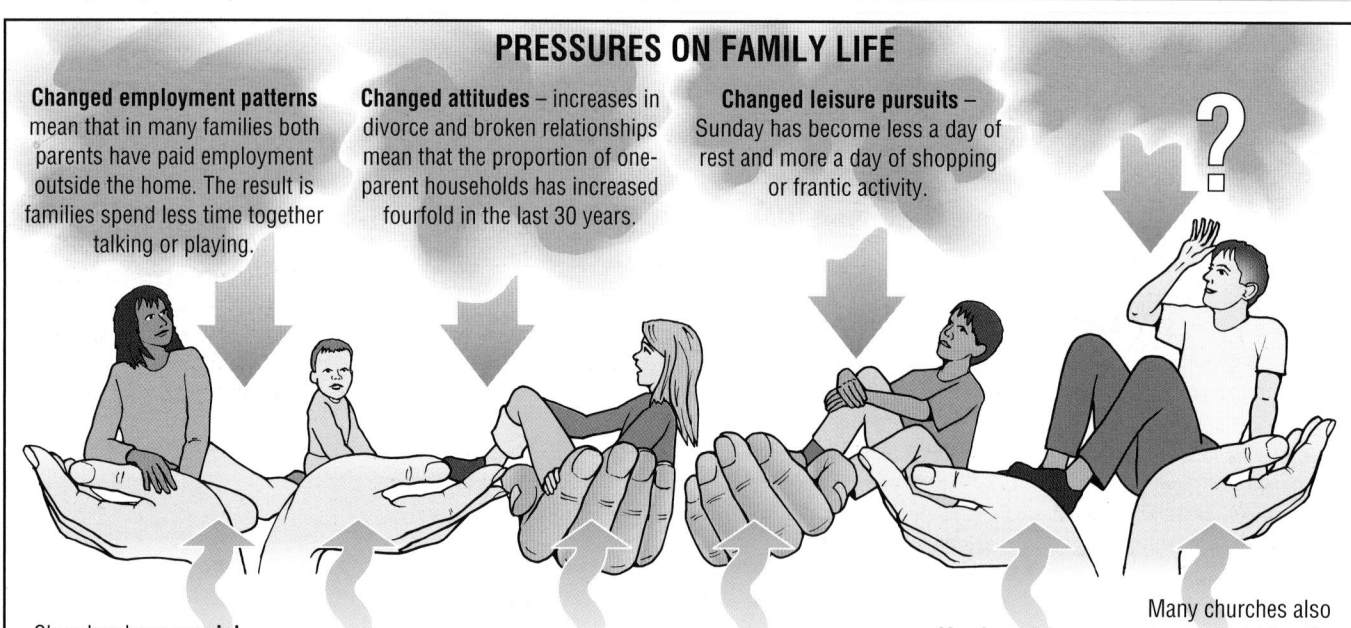

PRESSURES ON FAMILY LIFE

Changed employment patterns mean that in many families both parents have paid employment outside the home. The result is families spend less time together talking or playing.

Changed attitudes – increases in divorce and broken relationships mean that the proportion of one-parent households has increased fourfold in the last 30 years.

Changed leisure pursuits – Sunday has become less a day of rest and more a day of shopping or frantic activity.

Churches have **special services** following the birth of a baby (baptism or dedication) at which the parents and the church members promise to care for the child and bring him or her up to understand and follow Christian values.

Training and support – some churches run **parenting classes** to support and train Christian parents, plus other groups and activities.

Some churches run **schools** where they encourage a Christian ethos alongside the rest of the curriculum.

Youth work is an important part of many churches' weekly activities, including Sunday School classes, Girls' or Boys' Brigades, Cubs and Brownies, which teach Christian values.

Many churches also have special **family services** celebrating the family and doing activities which interest all ages together. Parties, outings and organised family activities are common features of church life.

CHURCH SUPPORT FOR CHRISTIAN FAMILY LIFE

◎ VIEWPOINTS: Family values

DISCUSS

1 Read Source R. Would you like to be part of the Wells family? Give reasons.

2 How can you tell from their family life that the Wells are a Christian family?

Having children and bringing up a family is a central purpose of Christian marriage. Source R introduces you to one Christian family. The Wells are members of a growing independent evangelical Church which started fourteen years ago on a new housing development near Nottingham. The Church meets in a school, or uses homes, pubs or hired rooms for its various activities. It devises its own services and is not connected with any 'denomination'. All the family help in the Church: Paul is the minister, Jane leads children's activities.

R

Paul

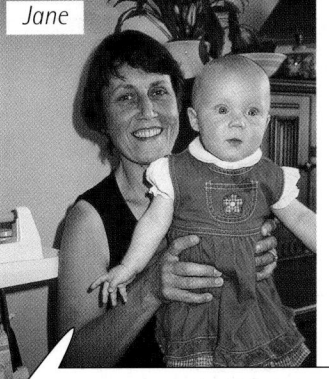

Jane

The Christian family is a tool to shape us. In the Bible God says to the Israelites, 'What you have learned from me, you should pass on to your children and your children's children.' We try to pass on our values. But Jane and I also change and grow from the experience of family life. Family life exposes all your weaknesses. What you are in the family is what you are! It's a chilling thought that we pass on what we are! Bringing up a family is the greatest responsibility most parents will ever have.

I don't like legalism. It's all about attitudes and perspective – having a God-like attitude to money, or your work, or the rest of your family. We don't tell our children do this or do that, we try to encourage them to reflect Christian values in their relationships with others – forgiveness, trust, etc. Young children might need do's and don'ts, but teenagers need their own clear and firm set of values to guide them in the decisions they have to make. We do a lot of things together. We try to keep Sunday special. We don't do any big shopping on Sundays – just emergencies. Sunday should not be just like any other day. In fact, at one service I suggested a minute's mourning silence for Nat West Bank because they had just opened the first Sunday bank.

I love children. I am sometimes tempted to hold on to them too tightly. I have to learn that they are God's and have to be handed back.

My family has always come first for me, but as they have got older I have been home-tutoring children excluded from school and I have also been fostering for the local authority. We had one family of three under-fives for 16 months, so you can imagine that this has to be a whole family commitment. Everyone has to support it. We prayed about it and agreed it together. Becky and Chris [their children] are brilliant with small children.

In difficult situations we try to listen to one another and see each other's point of view; we think about how Jesus would react in this situation. Using the Bible to make decisions is not about looking for a text in the Bible, but about thinking your way into what attitude Jesus would take.

Going to church together is very important. We've always done this. The children have always been involved. It's something we all share. But I think we still don't spend enough time together as a family. I don't think we discuss small decisions together enough.

As a family, we never let problems get out of hand. When we have arguments we try to forgive and forget quickly. We always try to sort out bad feelings before bedtime. Just praying together or reading the Bible as a family doesn't mean anything on its own. It's actions that count – hypocrites say all the right things but then don't do what God wants. We spend good time together: going to watch Notts County, church, meals, walking the dog, playing snooker.

The Wells family

FOCUS TASK

Here are some of the things the Wells listed as their family values:

- forgiveness and acceptance
- being ready to change
- thinking of others before yourself
- being honest with one another
- finding God's will.

1 Choose two values from the list and find examples in the statements of how this value affects the Wells' family life.

2 Draw or describe a pair of cartoons showing:
   a) family life without these values;
   b) family life with these values.

ISSUE : When marriages fail

Throughout the history of the Christian Church its leaders have had to recognise that Christians fall short of God's standards for marriage. Many marriages run into problems. What then?

Marriage guidance

Many Christians are deeply involved in marriage guidance counselling. They talk with couples whose relationships have problems and try to resolve them.

Many ministers, priests and Christian counsellors find that a large amount of time is spent helping people sort out marriage problems.

Divorce

Divorce is forbidden by some Christian traditions. The Catholic Church, for example, teaches that marriage is a 'sacrament', i.e. something made by God. No human agent has the right or the power to unmake something made by God. A divorce decree is therefore as meaningless as saying 'I was never born'; the couple were joined by God and nothing can unjoin them except death, although in extreme cases a marriage can be <u>annulled</u>. Churches that do not allow divorce train priests and counsellors to support couples whose marriages are failing.

Some Christian traditions do allow divorce. They see marriage as a contract or a covenant (see Checkpoint on page 36). It ought not to be broken but it can be, and provision must be made for this. According to the Old Testament, God hates divorce (Malachi 2.16). However, Jesus said that divorce was allowed, but only because the hardness of people's hearts made it inevitable that some marriages would not work (Matthew 19.8). In Sources U and V two Christians tell the stories of their divorces.

Divorce recovery

Some Churches have arranged divorce recovery workshops, where divorced Church members can talk through their experiences, learn from others who have been through similar experiences and be helped to build new lives.

Some Anglican priests have devised their own 'divorce services' to recognise the breakdown of a marriage, to mark its ending and release people from vows they are unable to fulfil. Revd Margaret Blackall drew on her own experience of divorce in writing the service she uses (see Source S). The Anglican synod was asked to approve such services for official Church use but has so far refused.

S

The service has confession, commitment and healing. There is also thanksgiving for what was good in the marriage, including the birth of children. When you come to a funeral, you are burying a body. A divorced person needs that experience of a funeral and the opportunity to say a goodbye.

Revd Margaret Blackall

Remarriage?

Some Churches allow divorcees to remarry in church, others do not. The Church of Scotland, for instance, remarries divorced people if the minister is convinced of their sincere commitment to the new relationship. Remarriage is seen as a sign of God's forgiveness and willingness to give people a new start.

The Church of England is still officially opposed to remarrying divorcees in church. Some people are campaigning for this to change. They argue that the most important Christian principles in this situation are **compassion** for the people who suffer because of a divorce, and **forgiveness** on all sides. The opponents say that to allow remarriage of divorcees undermines or devalues marriage.

DISCUSS

1 The law no longer requires one party to be at fault in a divorce. Is it helpful to use words like 'fault' when discussing marital breakdown?
2 Read Source S. Why do you think some clergy want such a service?
3 Why do you think it has not been accepted by the Bishops?
4 What are the arguments for and against such services being made available in Christian Churches?

DISCUSS

Source T is a joke but it is making a serious point. What point is it making?

T

THE BIG DAY — TRUE LOVE

O-kay! Can we have the bride's mother and stepfather with respective offspring by various couplings, the bride's father and his live-in-lover with their new baby, the groom's father and his partner Bob, his mother who took it badly at first but is over the worst, the chief bridesmaid who was engaged to the groom until so recently and her therapist, without whom she wouldn't be here today – good! Everybody happy?

U

I walked out on my violent husband after just two years of marriage. No one knew what it was like for me. I left with another man. I still believed that God was close to me, even if I had ignored his teaching. I had a responsible role in the local Church of England but twenty years on I still remember a member of the local Baptist church telling me, 'God will never use you again'. I got married again but in a Registry office, then there was a service of repentance and blessing in church. Unfortunately that marriage failed too, but I believe God has not abandoned me. Today I continue to be a leader in my local church and I feel close to God.

A woman Reader in the Church of England in her 40s

V

[After my divorce] one of the most difficult things to deal with was that I had stood up, in front of the people whom I loved the most, and before God, and made solemn promises, which I meant at the time, but which later I was unable to keep when I realised that this was not the right relationship for me. I felt very stupid and guilty and felt like a failure. I had let people down. I felt like a bad person. It takes a long time to get over these things.

I left the Church for a long time because I felt so guilty and out of place. I thought everyone was looking at me and seeing a bad person. I removed myself before they could get at me!

Now I am back at Church because the Church I go to is full of people who accept me for myself. They don't ask nosy questions about my past and they do not judge me for it.

A young woman, divorced after just two and a half years of marriage, explains her feelings about the divorce three years later.

ACTIVITY

1 On page 37 you wrote Five Golden Rules for a Christian marriage. Now write five more Golden Rules for a Christian approach to divorce. Bear in mind the experiences of the speakers in Sources U and V.

DISCUSS

2 Do you think that Christians largely agree or disagree about sex, marriage and family life? Explain your answer.
3 If society's attitudes change, should the attitudes of the Church change to fit in? Explain your answer.

FOCUS TASK

The Church wants a simple leaflet to give to school leavers explaining Christian ideas about relationships, sex, marriage and family life.

Work in groups to create a simple four-page leaflet giving information and guidance.

For some sections you might have to present alternatives for different traditions.

4.1
INTRODUCTION

What do Christians believe about prejudice and discrimination?

In this unit you will investigate two examples of prejudice and discrimination – racial discrimination and gender discrimination. But first of all look at the big picture.

✓ CHECKPOINT

Prejudice and discrimination

- PREJUDICE is an attitude. It means having an opinion which is not based on fact. For example, 'I think he won't do this job well because he is disabled.'
- DISCRIMINATION is an action. It means treating someone unfairly because of prejudice. For example, 'I won't employ him because he is disabled.'

In Britain today, many forms of discrimination are illegal. However, prejudice is not against the law, because an attitude cannot be made illegal.

➡ STARTER

1 Mr and Mrs Lucas are queuing up for the new film at the multiplex.

2 Suzanne is starting her course as a trainee garage mechanic.

3 Sheila is looking for a room to rent.

4 Donald has arrived at the shopping centre in his wheelchair.

5 Levi is applying for a job at the building society.

6 Rowan has just moved to a new school.

DISCUSS

In pairs discuss these cartoons.

1 If someone was being prejudiced in each picture, what would they be saying or thinking?
2 Discuss how you feel about each situation. Which example of prejudice do you feel is most serious or damaging and why?
3 Could anything be done to improve each situation? By whom?

SAVE AS ...

4 Explain the difference between prejudice and discrimination using examples from this page.

KEY CHRISTIAN BELIEFS: Prejudice and discrimination

Christians believe that prejudice and discrimination are wrong. They are against God's will. They damage human relationships. All Christian traditions agree about this even if Christians sometimes fail to practise what they preach. This diagram shows why.

What would Jesus do?

Christians get inspiration from the life of Jesus. Jesus lived in a time when there was much prejudice and discrimination. How did he deal with it?

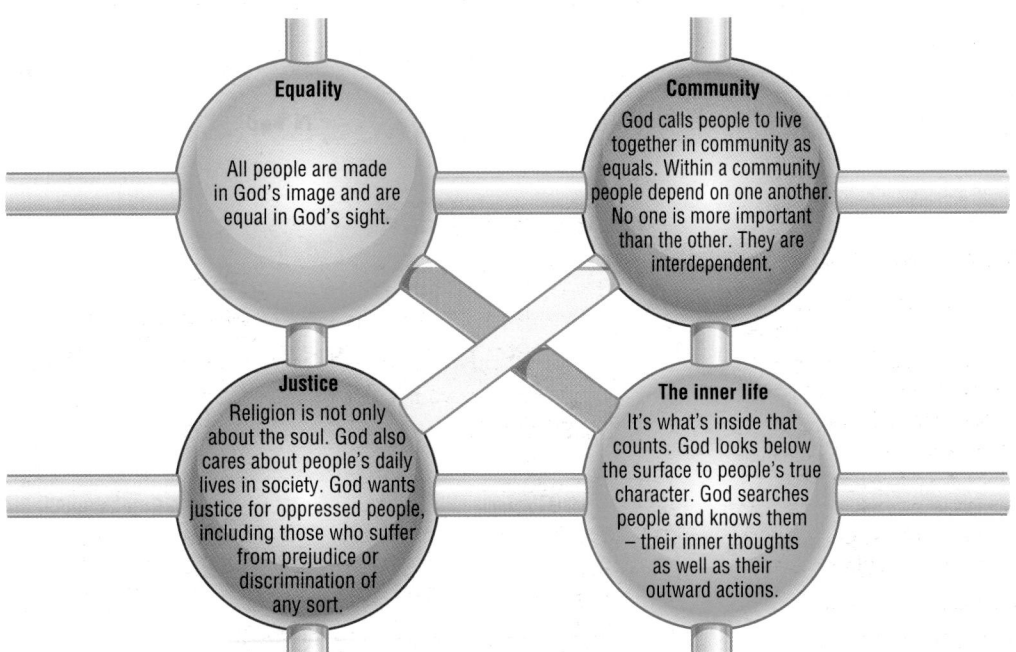

Equality
All people are made in God's image and are equal in God's sight.

Community
God calls people to live together in community as equals. Within a community people depend on one another. No one is more important than the other. They are interdependent.

Justice
Religion is not only about the soul. God also cares about people's daily lives in society. God wants justice for oppressed people, including those who suffer from prejudice or discrimination of any sort.

The inner life
It's what's inside that counts. God looks below the surface to people's true character. God searches people and knows them – their inner thoughts as well as their outward actions.

Luke 10.38–42 Martha and Mary
When Martha asked for Jesus to back her up and tell her sister off for sitting at Jesus' feet, listening to him teach, he doesn't. The custom of the day was that women should get on with housework, not be taught by rabbis, but Jesus says Mary chose wisely.

Luke 10.25–37 The Good Samaritan
Someone asked Jesus 'What must I do to go to heaven?' Jesus replied with this parable with a surprising ending. The Samaritan turns out to be the good guy. This is surprising because, as a race, Samaritans were hated by the Jews. Jesus tells people to go and do the same as the Samaritan. The key concept here is love for your neighbour whatever their background.

The example of Jesus

Galatians 3.26–28 All are equal
Here Paul is helping the first Christians follow the example of Jesus. Paul tells the Galatians that each of them is equal in Christ, whether a Jew or a Gentile, male or female, slave or free person. Christ is in all and makes everyone equal. The text sets aside prejudice based on gender, race, religion or social status.

Mark 2.15–17 Jesus and outcasts
Jesus mixed with many types of people: religious and non-religious; rich and poor; lepers, foreigners and political enemies. Religious leaders criticised him for this.

SAVE AS ...

Copy and complete this table. Leave column four blank to be completed as you work through this unit.

Bible passage	Type of prejudice being challenged	How challenged	Relevance today
Mark 2.15–17			
Luke 10.25–37			
Luke 10.38–42			
Galatians 3.26–28			

4.2

RACISM

How can Christians respond to racism?

All forms of prejudice and discrimination are damaging. But racism is a particular concern in modern Britain. In this unit you will investigate what the Christian Churches today are doing to challenge racism in society and in the Church itself. For your final task you will draw up an anti-racism policy for a church.

✓ CHECKPOINT

Multi-racial Britain

Britain has always had an ethnically mixed society.

However, over the past 50 years Britain has become much more racially diverse. After the Second World War Britain was short of workers and so people who lived in the British Commonwealth were invited to come to Britain to work. Many came particularly from the West Indies, India, Pakistan, Bangladesh and Hong Kong. According to the 2001 census 7.9 per cent of the population of Britain belongs to ethnic minorities; however, more than half of these are second generation – born and educated in Britain.

The Race Relations Act

In 1976 the government passed the Race Relations Act. This makes it unlawful to discriminate against anyone because of their race, colour, nationality or ethnic origin. It applies to all areas of life including jobs, housing and education. This is **civil** law. This means people have the right to take the discriminator to court and claim compensation if they are the victims of racial discrimination or harassment.

Racial violence or 'inciting racial hatred' are **criminal** offences. Such crimes can be investigated by the police. The person who commits them can be imprisoned.

Institutional racism

This means laws or practices that produce racial inequality even if the individuals who operate those laws don't intend to be racist.

➔ STARTER

A

Man half-blinded in racist attack

A Somalian man has lost the sight in one eye after being battered with an iron bar in what police say was 'a brutal racially-aggravated attack'.

The 40-year-old victim was attacked in Mare Street in Hackney, east London, in the early hours of Saturday morning. He was taken to an east London hospital where his condition was described as serious but stable.

Multiple injuries

Police said the man, from Bethnal Green, was approached by four white men who asked him for a cigarette. A police spokesman said the victim refused and the men started shouting racial abuse at him.

'The victim was punched and kicked to the ground and beaten with what we believe to be a metal bar or pole,' he said. Police said the victim was left lying on the pavement with multiple injuries to his face, head and body. He was found by a passer-by who called for an ambulance at 0500 GMT.

BBC News, 15 December 2002

B

More than half of Britons believe they live in a racist society, *according to a major survey commissioned by BBC News Online.*

- *44 per cent of those asked believe immigration has damaged Britain over the last 50 years.*
- *Racism in the workplace is a major problem with almost one in three blacks and Asians saying they believe racism has cost them the chance of a job.*
- *However most whites, blacks and Asians agree society is* **more** *racially tolerant than a decade ago.*

C

Would you consider marriage with someone of a different colour?
Yes 54% No 46%

Britain has more mixed-race marriages than any other country in Europe. And the majority of the population would be quite willing to marry someone of a different colour.

From 'Britain uncovered' poll, 2001

DISCUSS

Sources A–C are three news stories about Britain today.

a) How do they differ in their view of racism in Britain today?
b) Which do you think is the most accurate representation of race relations in Britain today?
c) Have you ever witnessed or been the victim of any sort of racism? If so explain what happened, what you felt and what you did about it.

KEY CHRISTIAN BELIEFS: Racism

Christianity is the largest worldwide religion. It has millions of members in all continents. It is a multiracial Church. It has ministers and leaders from all races.

There is widespread agreement among the Churches about racism. All the Christian Churches in Britain have made statements condemning racism – Source D is typical. They also agree about the reasons Christians should challenge and resist racism – see Diagram E. There is plenty in the Bible to support these ideas (see page 43 for example) but Story F gives one more specific example from the New Testament.

D

Racism has no part in the Christian Gospel. It contradicts our Lord's command to love our neighbours as ourselves. It offends the fundamental Christian belief that every person is made in the image of God and is equally precious. It solves no problems and creates nothing but hatred and fear.

George Carey, former Archbishop of Canterbury

E

*The human race is **one race** – created by one God for a common purpose*

*Racism is a human **sin** – to be repented of by individuals and by institutions*

*The human race is **diverse** – differences are significant and are to be celebrated*

*God wants justice **for the oppressed** – including those oppressed by racism*

F

Peter's vision (from Acts 10.1–35)

1 Peter doesn't want to accept Gentiles (non-Jews) into the Christian faith.

2 Peter has a vision.

3 In the blanket are all sorts of animals, reptiles and wild birds that his religion taught him are unclean.

4 God tells him 'Get up Peter; kill and eat'. Peter refuses. This happens three times then the vision ends.

5 I think God is trying to tell me something!

6 I now realise that it is true that God treats everyone on the same basis. Whoever worships him and does what is right is acceptable to him, no matter what race he belongs to.

SAVE AS ...

Write your own modern version of this story setting it in the present day. Your story should show someone coming to realise that God treats all people equally. What might their prejudice be at the start? What would happen in their dream? What would they do about it afterwards?

◉ ISSUE: How can Christians challenge racism?

Christianity may teach that all people are equal but individual Christians and churches have not always lived this out. Indeed there has been racism in the Church itself. Some black Christians felt excluded or undervalued in white-led churches. Some left the white-led churches to worship in black-led churches. Black-led or black-majority churches are the fastest growing churches in Britain today. But nowadays many Christians of all denominations consider it very important to challenge racism both within their own churches and in community life around them. They do this in different ways – some small scale, some large. Here are some examples:

G

My primary concern is not to turn up as a black person at yet another church service and to have white folks telling me how sorry they are, to wash my feet and to retrace the last 200 years of history. I want to know what are we going to do about racism **now** *and how are we going to construct a future which is one of mutual respect for all of us in 20 years' time.*

Rev Joel Edwards, General Director of the Evangelical Alliance, here involved on a community regeneration project in Peckham, South London.

> **A** Social events are the big opportunity to share food together, to share stories, to listen to each other, to laugh together.

> **B** The white community are a minority in this area of Newham but our church is still majority white. As part of **reaching out** to the majority Asian community around us (mainly Bengali) we help run literacy classes, particularly for women who need to learn English.

> **C** We ran a series of **special services** focusing on the different countries represented in our congregation. At one of them we laid all the chairs out in the shape of the sweep of the islands of the Caribbean – so everyone was sitting on a different island. They had to find one member of the congregation who had a connection with that island and find out more about it.

> **D** For Jubilee 2000 (a campaign to cancel the debt of the poorest nations) we joined the march in Birmingham and it was the first event which really got both black and white members of our church **involved together** in taking political action. It also united young and old and rich and poor and men and women in a shared goal.

DISCUSS

H

There's this young white lad who read both the Bible readings during the service last week. I've only seen him here once before and there he was out at the front reading the lessons. And people noticed. When he walked out the front, Jean looked at Mavis, Mavis looked at me and I looked at the floor. You know, hardly ever is a black person called out to do anything at the front. It's like they don't even think to ask if any of us would like to do anything. It's not that we always want to be at the front. Just that we'd like the opportunity to turn it down if we wanted to. It's obvious and so hurtful.

Michelle, in her 40s

1 Read Source H. In what ways are people being racist?

2 How could a church deal with this situation?

3 How might the following passages in the Bible help a Christian person to react appropriately to this situation:

- Matthew 6.14–15
- Mark 2.15–17?

4 Study the four strategies shown in the bubbles on this page.
  a) In what ways are people challenging racism in each example?
  b) Which do you think is the most effective way of challenging racism? Put the actions in order of effectiveness (in your view) and explain your order.

CASE STUDY: Bishop John Sentamu

John Sentamu is Bishop of Birmingham. He was a lawyer and judge in Uganda until 1975. When he was just 25, John Sentamu was among the tens of thousands who fled the country, when Idi Amin, President of Uganda, started a reign of terror against his own people. John Sentamu came to Britain. He became a minister in the Church of England in 1979. Over the next 20 years he rose quickly to become the first senior black bishop.

John Sentamu has been closely involved in investigating racism in British society. He served on the Church of England's inquiry into racism in the Church itself.

The inquiry found:

- ❏ a lack of black leaders
- ❏ a lack of participation by black church members in the activities of the churches
- ❏ a belief that racism is only an issue in inner city areas where people from ethnic minorities tend to live.

He got involved in two high profile inquiries. While he was Bishop of Stepney he headed the inquiry into the death of Damilola Taylor in 2000 which many people suspected was a racially motivated attack. He was also involved in the inquiry into the death of Stephen Lawrence who was murdered in a racist attack by five white men in 1993. He believes the Church not only needs to sort out its own racism but also must take an active part in challenging racism in society. For example:

> We called our report 'The Passing Winter' because many black people had been frozen out of the Church. The winter is passing but it still has not gone. There are still people with racist attitudes, racist views or racist ideas. The Church of England was built on the basis that anything white is normal so it tended to have a built-in bias against black people. But the Church of England has been quite brave in admitting its racism. It has been more honest than society at large about what is going on. And it has been quite clear: everybody is made in God's image, of equal worth.

> The Church of England has churches in every police area so our church buildings could be offered as neutral centres where racist incidents and crimes can be reported, information exchanged between police and community groups, surveys carried out, and training given.

> No one is born a racist. Racism is caught, learned, taught, imitated, and then practised. It can be rooted out.

DISCUSS

These are some of the practical measures considered by the Church of England for dealing with racism in the church.

The diagram has two empty spaces. Work with a partner to add two more based on the information on the last four pages.

- All Church schools to help their pupils experience and value different cultures
- Send bishops and church leaders on racism awareness courses
- Set recruitment quotas for black clergy and teachers at Church schools

Dealing with racism

SAVE AS...

The Christian response to racism can be summarised in three words:

- Diverse – so celebrate differences rather than ignoring them
- Equal – treating each other as equals in the sight of God
- Together – joint activities that draw Christians together as a community towards a shared goal.

For each activity in your diagram add an explanation:
a) why it might help challenge racism
b) how it relates to one of these key ideas: diverse, equal, together.

Images of Jesus

J

Christ depicted in a painting by Edward A. Armitage (1869)

ACTIVITY

Study Sources I–P.

1 Write down the messages about Jesus that you think each image portrays.
2 Which image comes closest to the way you picture Jesus?
3 Which image do you think comes closest to the real appearance of Jesus?
4 No one knows what Jesus actually looked like. Is this an advantage or a disadvantage to Christians who are fighting racism?

I

An orthodox mosaic of Jesus from the 11th century

K

The Baptism of Christ by a modern Haitian artist

L

Tattoo, Miami, Florida 1997

O

T-shirt, Edinburgh, Scotland 2003

M

Face of Jesus painted on African skirt, Paris 1997

N

Sandals printed with pictures of Jesus and Mary, Copenhagen, Denmark 2003

P

The Arrest of Christ, Gospel of St Matthew from the Book of Kells, c.800

FOCUS TASK

Racism is not only morally unacceptable, it is also illegal in many cases. The British law makes it an offence to incite racial hatred or to discriminate on the grounds of race.

Every school has to have an equal opportunities policy to ensure that they are fighting racism in the classroom and in the school organisation. Maurice Hobbs of the group Evangelical Christians for Racial Justice argues that churches should also have equal opportunities policies.

Working in groups, create a statement summarising Christian attitudes to racism which could be included in a local church's anti-racism policy. It should set out:

• Christian principles that lie behind the Church's opposition to racism
• how those principles can be applied to fighting racism in a church and its locality.

You could use this format suggested by Maurice Hobbs:

We believe that ... therefore ...

Your teacher can give you an example from a real church to help you.

Are women treated as equals in Christianity?

Your exam may need you to refer to two different examples of prejudice and discrimination. So this feature spread focuses on the issue of sexual discrimination.

➡ STARTER

ACTIVITY

1 Look at Source A. The cartoon Moses **is** making this up! But sometimes it is harder to tell. Here are six statements about women (1–6). Five of them are real, one is made up. See if you can work out which is which. Your teacher can tell you if you are right.

2 Many people would find these opinions amusing but also offensive:

a) Explain how these quotations from Christian men fail to treat women with either justice or equality.

b) Why do you think they said those things?

c) How would you respond to them?

A

1

Women are simple souls who like simple things, and one of the simplest is the simplest to give ... Our family Airedale will come clear across the yard for one pat on the head. The average wife is like that. She will come across town, across the house, across the room, across to your point of view, and across almost anything to give you her love if you offer her some honest approval.

Episcopal Bishop James Pike in 1968

2

Women should remain at home, sit still, keep house, and bear and bring up children ... If a woman grows weary and at last dies from childbearing, it matters not. Let her die from bearing – she is there to do it.

Martin Luther, 1483–1546

3

If God had wanted women to be in charge he would have made them bigger and taller and stronger than men. As it is, the way God created man and woman shows that he intended men to rule, women to obey.

John Joseph, writing a problem page in a Christian magazine in the 1950s

4

Women should keep quiet in the meetings. If women want to find out about something they should ask their husbands at home. It is a disgraceful thing for a woman to speak in church.

The Bible: St Paul writing to the Christians in Corinth, first century CE

5

In the year 584 there was a council of the church in Mâcon, France. There was a long debate on the question, 'Are women human?' After a vote, women were declared to be human by 32 votes to 31.

6

Adam was tempted by Eve, not she by him. It is right that he whom woman led into wrongdoing should have her under his direction, so that he may not fail a second time through female weakness.

Gratian, a church leader writing in 1140

CHECKPOINT

Sex Discrimination Act

The Sex Discrimination Act was introduced in Britain in 1975. This made it illegal to discriminate against men or women on the grounds of sex. It particularly focuses on employment. It became illegal for an employer to exclude someone from a job purely because of their sex. It also dealt with many other areas of life including education, provision of goods and services, and advertising.

It strengthened the Equal Pay Act of 1970, which stated that women could not be paid less than men for performing the same work.

Women's ordination

Ordination means becoming a minister or priest. The Orthodox and Catholic Churches do not ordain women as priests. Most of the Protestant Churches do, although this is a recent development. The Church of England only started in 1992 and there are still some who regard this as a big mistake.

Some people argue that the Catholic Church is guilty of sex discrimination in not allowing women to become priests. However a section of the Act exempts organised religions if a job is restricted to one sex to **comply with doctrine** or to **avoid offending its followers**.

★ KEY CHRISTIAN BELIEFS: Sexism

The views on the opposite page are undoubtedly sexist. Historically, the Church does not have a good record on sexism. Indeed some would say that Christianity has long treated women as second-class citizens and some traditions still do so. They use Bible passages such as 1 Timothy 2.8–15 to support their view that men should lead and women should raise children. However, nowadays Christians are much more likely to emphasise:

Men and women may be different but …

… they are equal before God …
As Paul **says**:
'Through faith all of you are God's children … So there is no difference between men and women – you are all one in union with Christ Jesus.' Galatians 3.26–28.

… and the church should value women more
Women see the world in a different way from men. They also tend to be more caring and accepting and good at compromising than men. It is good that God created men and women with different characters. This female perspective enriches the Church and the Church must value it and use it much more.

… and women should have similar opportunities to men
… to have a career, to lead in the Church, to make the big decisions and should not be stereotyped as mothers or home-makers. However, some denominations have stopped short of allowing women to become priests.

Or as Jesus **showed** by his actions:
He included women among his closest companions and treated women with respect whenever he met them. He sometimes went against the conventions of his time which kept men and women separate.

B

*God our Mother
You hold our life within you,
nourish us at your breast,
and teach us not to walk alone.
Help us so to receive your tenderness
And respond to your challenge
that others may draw life from us
in your name.*
Janet Morley in the *SPCK Book of Christian Prayer*

C

Women are involved in nearly all spheres of life; they ought to be permitted to play their part fully [in the Church] according to their own particular nature...
Vatican 2 – a set of teachings which guide the Catholic Church on various moral and social issues

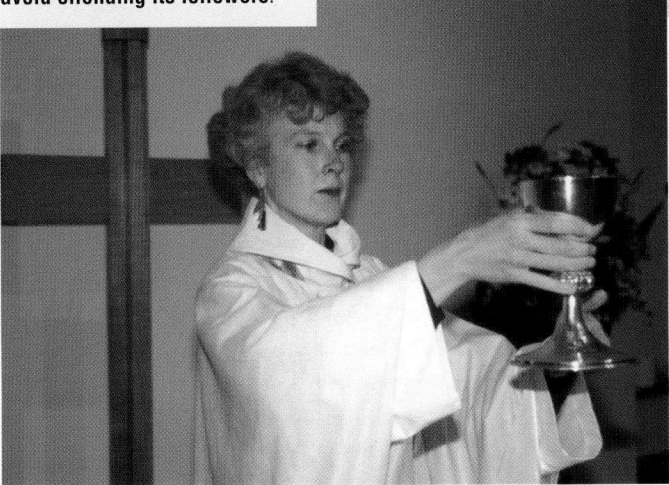
Rev Catherine Rumens blessing the elements for Holy Communion

ACTIVITY

Read Source B to ten people and note down their responses. What conclusions do you draw from your findings?

FOCUS TASK

'It is much more important to root out racism in society than to root out sexism in the Church.'

Do you agree? Explain your view showing you have considered other points of view.

5.1

INTRODUCTION

How can individuals change the world?

The problems of the world are beamed onto our televisions every day and many people feel helpless when faced by them. However, we are probably not as helpless as we think we are! It is possible, with the communications available through travel, trade, media and information technology, to influence the world for the better. Decisions we make today can affect some of these issues! This unit investigates some of these issues and Christian responses to them.

 STARTER

A

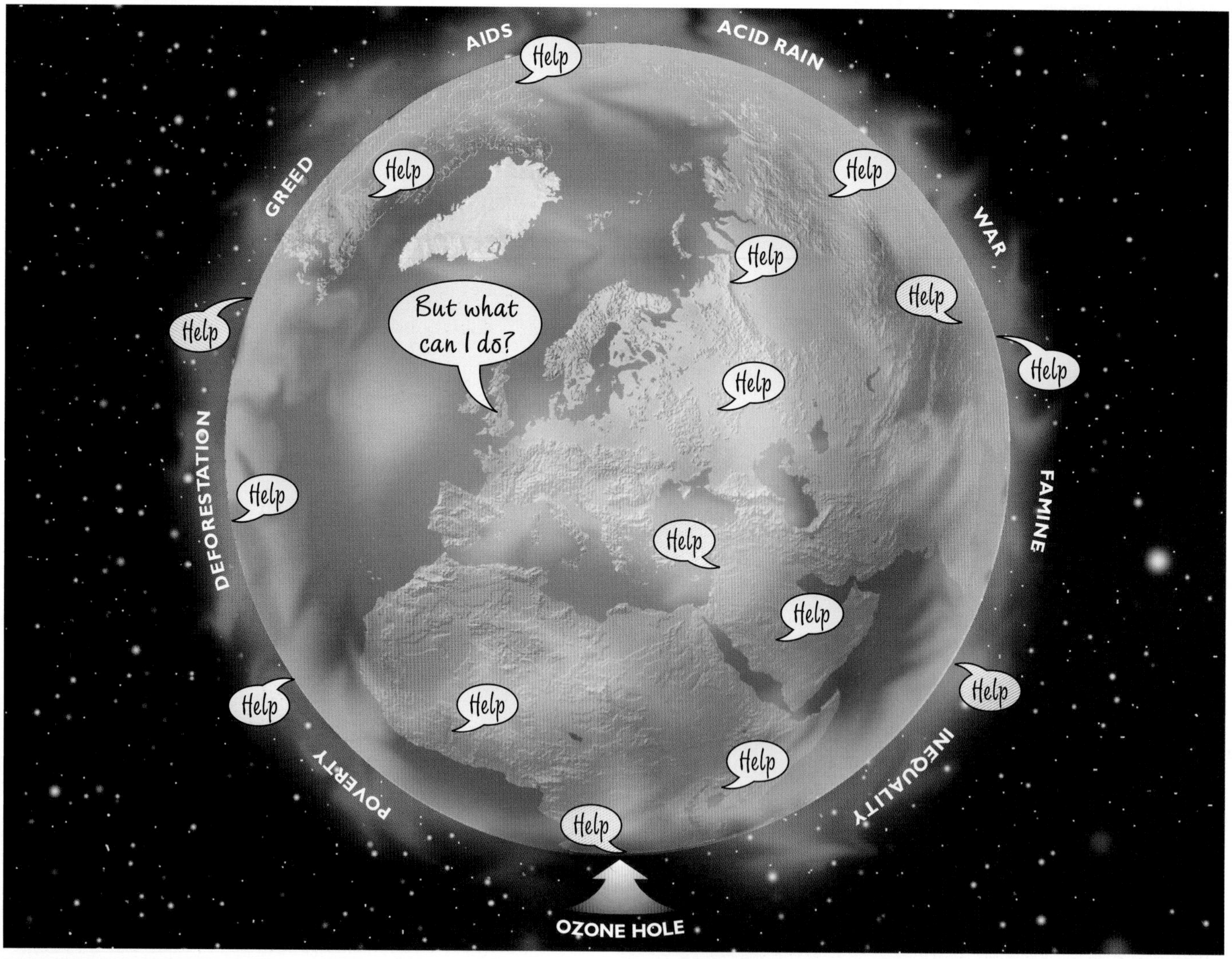

DISCUSS

This cartoon shows a number of world issues.

- Are there any issues you would want to add?
- Which of the problems in this cartoon do you think is the most serious?

B

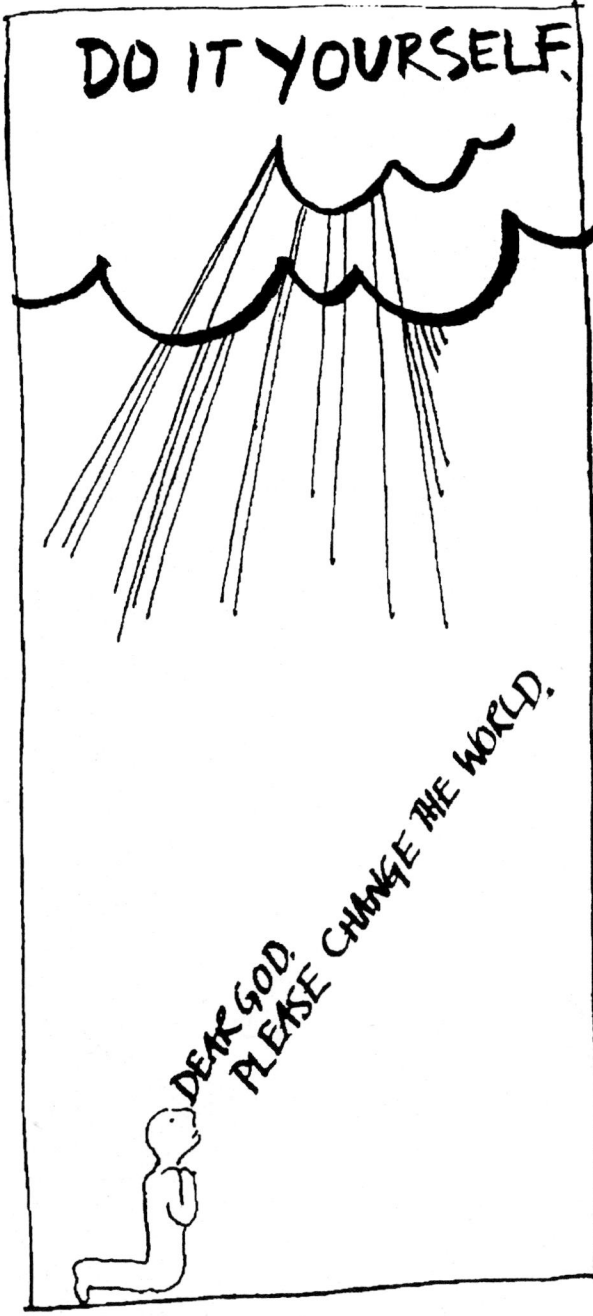

C

Messiah Man

I am getting weary from listening to deceit
From people in a hurry to change my society
I and I a victim of Babylon history
Political immorality has taken my memory

Wise man say the system never shall change
Jah man say until the people have changed
My people live in sorrow, no food for the children to eat
No hopes for a better tomorrow and this is to say the least

Messiah is watching over your activities
Soon he is returning to judge all your practices
Wise man say the system never shall change
Jah man say until the people have changed,
people have changed

I say we need Messiah Man

From *Messiah Man* by Ben Okafor

D

Christ has no body now on Earth but yours, no hands but yours, no feet but yours. Yours are the eyes through which Christ's compassion is to look out on the world. Yours are the feet with which he is doing good. Yours are the hands with which he is to bless others now.

St Teresa of Avila, writing more than 400 years ago

E

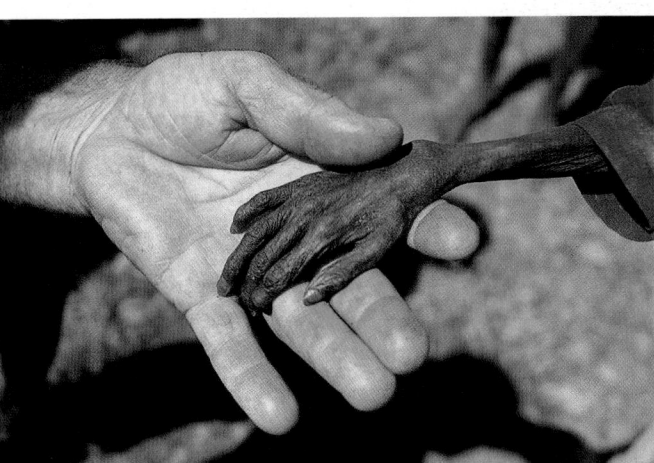

This photograph, taken in Uganda in 1980, shows a Catholic priest holding the hand of a starving Ugandan child during a famine caused by civil war in that country.

DISCUSS

1 a) Are the cartoon (B), the poem (C) and the meditation (D) making the same point?
  b) What point or points are they making?
2 How do you respond to Source E?
3 a) Do you think **you** can change the world? Why? Why not?
  b) Do others agree with you? Why? Why not?

SAVE AS …

4 Write a paragraph to record the views of your class on how far individuals can change the world.

How should Christians help the poor?

Most Christians agree about the need to help the poor. But they don't always agree about how to do it. In this investigation you will look at different Christian attitudes to wealth and poverty. For your focus task you will draw up five golden rules to help Christians decide how to use their money, and particularly how to use their money to help the poor.

✅ CHECKPOINT

MEDCs and LEDCs

Countries of the world are often divided into MEDCs (More economically developed countries) and LEDCs (Less...). Britain, the USA and much of Europe are MEDCs. Almost everyone living in an MEDC has access to enough food, water and housing to meet their basic needs and usually the government helps individuals who are too poor to cope on their own. In MEDCs there is usually free education, good health care and low infant mortality. They have the money to cope when things go wrong. There are often still great inequalities between rich and poor but most of the population has enough money to live.

Many more countries in the world are LEDCs. In these countries there is often only basic education and poor health care, lots of babies die at birth, and there is often a risk of severe famine and starvation if crops fail. Such countries are often stuck in a vicious circle that keeps them poor. They don't have enough money to start educating their population which might then help them develop. This can be made even worse if they are involved in wars.

Jubilee 2000: debt cancellation

One particular problem for LEDCs is that they often also owe a lot of money to MEDCs. Sometimes they borrowed this money 30 or 40 years ago but are still paying the interest even if they can't afford to pay back the money. Some poor countries are paying the rich countries more in interest than they receive in aid so they are getting poorer instead of richer.

The Jubilee 2000 campaign was set up by the churches and others to call on governments in rich countries to cancel the debt of the poor countries so they can start with a clean slate. In 2000, the British government announced that all debt payments to the UK from 41 of the poorest countries had been stopped or would be held in trust, to be returned one day to fund poverty reduction. However, a lot of the money is not owed to governments but to private banks so governments cannot cancel those debts.

DISCUSS

Work with a partner to discuss your reactions to the window (Source A).

1 Why do you think some Christians might wish to have this stained-glass window in their church?

2 Why might other people not think this is appropriate?

3 What do you think? Is this a good or a bad image to have in a church? Why?

➔ STARTER

A

A stained-glass window in St Mary's Church, Bishop Auckland, Northumberland

KEY CHRISTIAN BELIEFS: Wealth and poverty

Why do Christians help those in need?

All Christian traditions would agree that it is a Christian duty to help the poor. Many different sources of authority point Christians towards this responsibility. For example:

Church teaching. All traditions emphasise the need to help the poor. They give money to agencies that help the poor, or set up such agencies. As part of the influential *Vatican 2* (see page 97) the Catholic Church decided that it should be closely involved with poor people's struggle for justice. *Vatican 2* sent a signal from the Catholic leadership that allowed the Liberation Theology movement to develop in Catholic communities around the world (see page 60).

The Bible. Much of the Old Testament law is designed to protect the poor. The Old Testament prophets call for **justice** and **compassion** for the poor. In the New Testament, Jesus loves the poor and has compassion for them. He praises those who help the poor; he condemns those who do nothing for them. Much of Jesus' teaching is concerned with **stewardship**. The good steward is one who uses what they have been given or what they have earned wisely or well. Using wealth wisely and well, according to Jesus, means using it to show compassion.

Why help the poor?

Individual conscience. This is a powerful motivation to help the poor. Christians may be moved to action by hearing the story of an ordinary human being struggling in poverty. Their conscience stimulates them to take action.

Christian leaders. Some of the most widely respected Christian leaders of the past and present are those most closely identified with helping the poor, such as Martin Luther King in the USA (see page 69). The example and teaching of others inspires Christians to try to help the poor.

DISCUSS

Read the account in Source B.

1 Why do you think the young woman chose the minister's house?

2 Do you think the minister was right to turn the young woman away? Give your reasons.

SAVE AS ...

3 Look up the following passages from the Bible:

1 Timothy 6.6–10   Luke 21.1–4   Matthew 19.16–22

Copy and complete this diagram. Alongside each reference write some notes to summarise the main idea of that passage. Add to your diagram as you work through this unit. Use the blank spaces to add further Bible references and their explanations. There are references on pages 58, 59 and 60.

4 Write your own one-sentence summaries of the following key words, recording their meaning for Christians. You might also find the glossary helpful.

  a) Justice

  b) Compassion

  c) Stewardship

B

One cold evening in winter, a young woman knocked on our door. She was covered in a blanket and shivering. She begged my father, the local minister, for enough money to get to a hostel by bus. He refused, as he refused all people who came to our house because he was worried that if word got around, every tramp and vagrant in the local area would be running to our front door. My mum once let someone in for bread and soup. Dad was really cross when he found out.

CASE STUDY: How does Christian Aid fight poverty?

We believe in life before death

Christian Aid was formed in Britain and Ireland as the Second World War was coming to an end. It was originally set up to help refugees and churches recover from the war. Gradually the work of the organisation grew to help meet different needs in dozens of countries all around the world. Thirty-nine Churches in the United Kingdom and Ireland are now part of Christian Aid. Its income is around £60 million. This is raised through fundraising activity, such as door-to-door collection in Christian Aid Week, through various grants and through donations from member Churches, supporters and the general public.

C

- 16% campaigning and education
- 19% fundraising and publicity
- 2% management and administration
- 52% development
- 11% emergencies

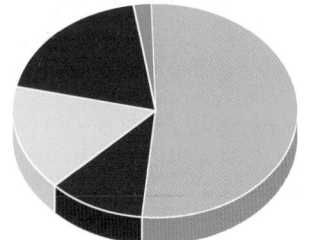

How Christian Aid spends its money

SAVE AS ...

Using the example of the Deccan Development Society, explain in your own words the difference between:

a) disaster relief
b) development work.

Development work = helping the poor to help themselves

Christian Aid responds to emergencies when they happen. However, the bulk of its work is 'development work' – long-term, small-scale projects run locally. These projects help people to help themselves, so they no longer have to depend on help from outside, and include strengthening communities to cope with future emergencies. This is known as sustainable development.

This includes helping people get access to clean water; learn to read and write; and develop sustainable farming methods. One example is the Deccan Development Society (the DDS) in Central South India (see Source D). Once financial help and legal advice have been given to start the project, Christian Aid expects the DDS to run itself and be self-financing. Christian Aid does not provide foreign experts or expensive modern technology. This is inappropriate. Development work needs to build the skills and power of the local people.

D

Anishama is working for the Deccan Development Society in the village of Indoor. She is teaching members of the local women's sangham (council) about new farming methods which can produce more food and reduce environmental damage. She is demonstrating how to contour the land to prevent erosion.

Campaigns = changing the policies that hold back the poor

Christian Aid argues that poverty is often caused, or made worse, by government policies in Britain and other developed countries. For example, in past decades Western governments and banks lent billions of pounds to developing countries who cannot now repay the debts. The interest they have to pay on these debts drains wealth from the developing countries. So Christian Aid and other development agencies campaign for such debts to be cancelled so poor countries can spend the money on solving their own problems.

However, some Christians worry about such policies, which they feel are too 'political'. Christian Aid would not deny they are political; they would say that applying Christianity in these situations means you have to be 'political'. However, Christian Aid is not party-political. It calls on all parties to support policies which help alleviate poverty.

DISCUSS

Source E shows two examples of Christian Aid's campaigns. Which campaign do you think would be more likely to succeed? Why?

E

Extracts from some of Christian Aid's recent campaigns

Fair Trade

Christian Aid also argues that helping the poor means changing the way the world trades. People in rich  countries import a lot of food and other goods made in poorer countries but only a tiny portion of the price people pay in the rich countries goes to the producers and workers that made it or grew it. The rest goes in profit to the international companies. Christian Aid encourages its supporters to support the Fair Trade movement which tries to help producers get a fair price for their goods by buying direct from farmers in LEDCs and ensuring that workers on those farms are well looked after. Lots of companies claim that their goods are fairly traded but only goods with this mark have been checked out by the Fair Trade Foundation and proved to be Fair Traders.

ACTIVITY

> Why don't you do something about the problems here in Britain? We've got enough of them.

> Christian Aid is far too political. What about these people's spiritual needs?

> I prefer to give to non-religious charities.

> These people need to learn to stand on their own two feet.

Study the statements above. These were reasons given for not supporting Christian Aid during a door-to-door collection. How would you respond if you were a Christian Aid collector? Explain your answer with reference to:

a) the information about Christian Aid
b) Christian beliefs about helping the poor.

You could role-play a conversation on the doorstep.

⊙ ISSUE: Should Christians be rich?

> Yes, if they use their wealth wisely and well.

John Laing

John Laing in 1962 (above) and one of his company's building sites today (below)

John Laing was brought up in a Christian home, where he went to church every week. His father was a builder who owned a small firm, which John joined at fifteen, when he left school. He spent three years learning how to be a builder, before he could join his father in managing the business. John was ambitious; he wanted his father to try building bigger and more exciting things. The Laing Company usually built houses; John wanted them to expand and build factories, reservoirs and hospitals. Slowly he persuaded his father to try working on larger projects. First they built a reservoir, and then they started building sewers by the docks in Barrow-in-Furness. John worked out carefully the costs involved in the build but disaster struck. First the building site was flooded, then they had to dig through quicksand to build the sewers. But things got worse when the owners decided to take Laing to court, and ask for compensation, because the project was not completed on time. John was afraid that their company would be made bankrupt, all because of his desire for the company to do bigger projects. One day he sat with his head in his hands and prayed, 'God, I have had enough, because I've been so ambitious I have almost ruined the business and have worried my parents in their old age. Please show me a way through these problems. If the company survives I promise I will run it differently in the future. I will think and pray about which projects to accept and pray you will guide me into making better decisions. Amen.'

A little while later the Laing Company won the court case; instead of celebrating, John found some writing paper and wrote his 'Programme of Life'. There were two parts to it:

1 Being a Christian was the most important thing in his life. This meant reading the Bible, praying to God and going to church would always be more important to him than his business.

2 He decided that he wanted to make sure he enjoyed life and wanted to help others to enjoy life too.

At the same time, he thought about how he would spend his money. He decided that just because he might earn more and more money, he did not have to spend it on himself. He decided he would live on a small amount and then give money away to people who were hungry, to charities and to his church. The rest of the money he would reinvest into the business or into charities.

In the 1920s builders did not have pensions or paid holidays. John did not agree with this, so he set up a company holiday scheme and was the first person to introduce a pension scheme into the building trade. He wasn't just interested in the company making profit but in treating people well.

By the 1950s the Laing Company employed over 15 000 workers; John and his family could have been very rich indeed. But John always lived by his 'Programme of Life' and gave away a lot of his money secretly. Lots of churches, missionaries and other organisations have received money from him, many never knowing it came from John Laing. For example, he quietly provided most of the money for London Bible College to be built and established.

After a long and busy life, John died in 1978 at the age of 98. He had made millions of pounds and he had chosen to give most of it away. When he died he owned only £371, probably less than most of the people who had worked for him. His love for God was more important to him than money and his life had proved it.

Adapted from *Building to Share – The Story of John Laing* by Deborah Helme

DISCUSS

1 Look up Matthew 9.16–18. How has John Laing put this teaching into practice?
2 Using wealth wisely and well is called 'good stewardship'. What evidence is there that John Laing has been a 'good steward'.
3 Do you approve of the way he has chosen to spend his money? Explain your answer. Suggest causes you would support if you were John Laing.
4 'Money cannot buy happiness'. Do you think this is true? Give more than one point of view.

> No, wealth and possessions should be shared.

The Iona Community

In 1938 George MacLeod founded a Christian community on the tiny island of Iona off the west coast of Scotland.

Clergymen and helpers gave up time and money to learn building, carpentry and stone-masonry, and together they rebuilt Iona's ruined abbey.

The George MacLeod Centre was later opened to provide a place where young people from across the world could come and live for a time in a community. They contribute to practical tasks like cleaning, cooking and gardening. In the summer volunteers look after visitors as guides or shop-workers. When they are not working they follow a regular pattern of worship and study as well as enjoying the company of other people within the community.

The people who live in the community do so because they believe that a life shared with others is better than one where people are on their own as individuals or in small family clusters. Community members come from all walks of life and are drawn to Iona for personal or spiritual reasons. Their life is relatively simple. No one is really rich in material possessions but no one has to endure real poverty. You can see what the island looks like today in Source F.

The Iona Community does not just worry about its own affairs. Most Community members live and work away from Iona, in deprived areas of Scotland. Some support Church of Scotland projects in the poorest parts of Glasgow. Others are at work in the wider world. These members of the Community return to Iona for one week per year. They give a proportion of their income to the Community. The Iona Community has led anti-nuclear protests and campaigns against what they regard as unjust government policies. Worship in the Iona Community focuses on social concerns around the world. This is reflected in daily prayers, such as Source G.

F

Front cover of Iona's programme showing the island and the abbey.

G

Here is a gaping sore, Lord:
half the world diets,
the other half hungers;
half the world is housed,
the other half homeless;
half the world pursues profit,
the other half senses loss.
Redeem our souls, redeem our peoples,
redeem our times.

A prayer by John Bell, of the Iona Community

DISCUSS

1 Look up Acts 2.44–47. How have the Iona community put this teaching into practice?
2 How would you like living in a community, sharing everything you owned?
3 How likely is it that shared possessions would make some people in the community lazy?
4 What effect do you think prayers like Source G have?

Explain your answers to these questions.

FOCUS TASK

1 Work in groups. Draw up a set of guidelines or five Golden Rules to help all Christians decide how to use their money. At least two of your rules should be supported with reference to a passage from the Bible.
2 Now work on your own. Write a paragraph to explain how far you think these rules are good guidance for your own attitude to wealth and poverty. Explain your reasons.

ISSUE: Liberation Theology

H

The spirit of the Lord is upon me, because he has chosen me to bring good news to the poor. He has sent me to proclaim liberty for the captives and recovery of sight to the blind; to set free the oppressed, and announce that the time has come when the Lord will save his people.

Luke 4.18–19. Jesus begins his public ministry by quoting the prophet Isaiah.

In the 1960s many countries in Latin America were military dictatorships. These regimes were often brutal and corrupt. They ignored basic human rights, took the best land and industries for their own profit, murdered their own citizens, and followed economic policies that made the poorest poorer and the richest richer. A tiny minority lived in luxury, while the vast majority lived in abject poverty. Anyone who questioned the rulers was branded a communist and was likely to be killed.

Out of this situation developed a way of thinking about God and religion which became known as Liberation Theology. This sees God as a liberator who sets people free, who sides with the poor, who hates injustice.

I

Jesus is God, Man and Woman standing in firm solidarity ... This is a God who is sensitive to suffering.

Luz Beatriz Arellano, a Nicaraguan Christian and feminist

J

When you made this universe at the beginning of time, you wanted a world where the strong did not oppress the weak, where injustice did not conquer truth, where rich and poor shared their food equally. But we confess, O God, that we have turned your beautiful creation into a world of corruption and death, where the poor are oppressed and justice is crushed. Forgive us, God, and teach us how to live according to your wishes. Amen.

A Latin-American prayer

K

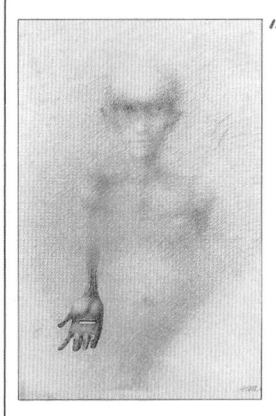

"When I give food to the poor, they call me a saint.

When I ask why the poor have no food, they call me a communist."

– Dom Helder Camara

Helder Camara is a Brazilian Catholic theologian and priest. He has been a champion of the poor and of non-violent social change in Brazil, and worldwide, through *Vatican 2* (see page 97). Communism is a system of government where wealth is shared out by the government.

DISCUSS

1 Write three ways in which you think that a Christian saying the prayer in Source J could back it up with practical action.
2 Use the information on this page to explain in your own words the message of Source K.
3 Read the story strip on page 61. What would **you** do if you were a Christian in El Salvador?
4 **Why** would you do it?

Some Christians went even further and joined armed struggle (see page 68).

The life and death of Oscar Romero

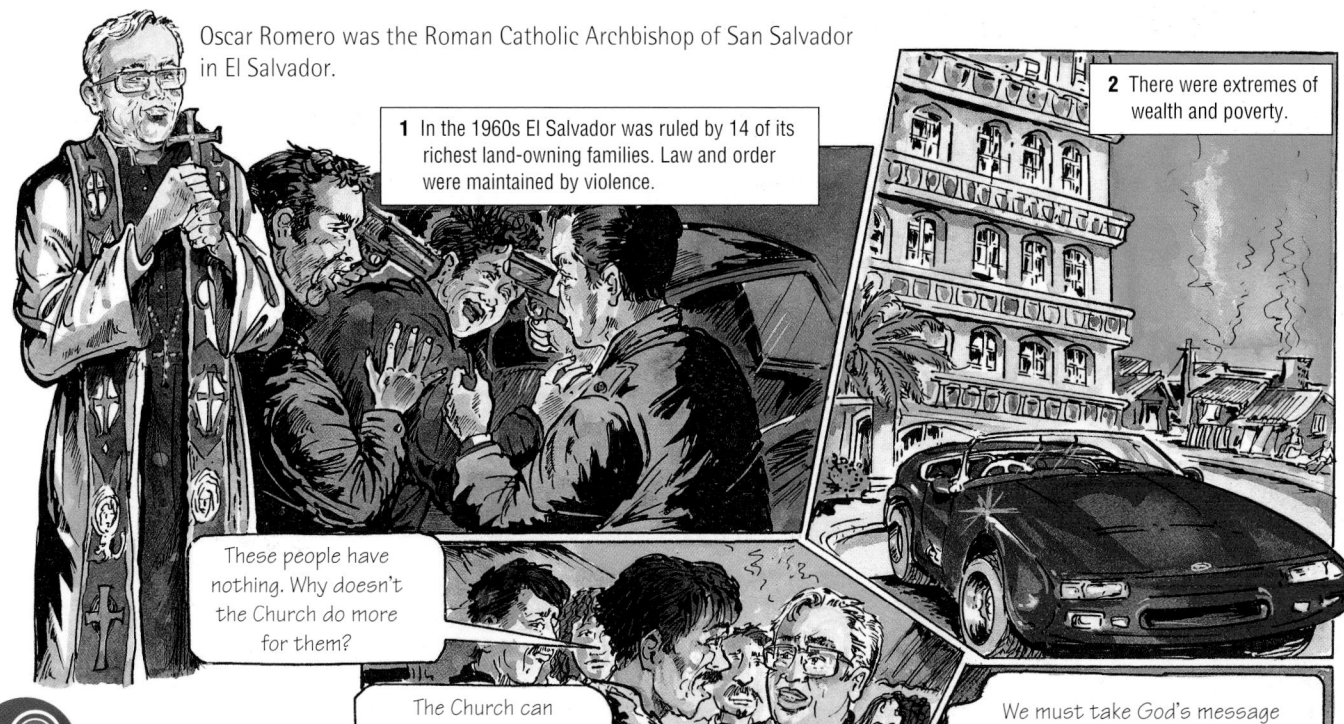

Oscar Romero was the Roman Catholic Archbishop of San Salvador in El Salvador.

1 In the 1960s El Salvador was ruled by 14 of its richest land-owning families. Law and order were maintained by violence.

2 There were extremes of wealth and poverty.

These people have nothing. Why doesn't the Church do more for them?

The Church can serve the poor, but it cannot challenge the way things are – that's not our job.

We must take God's message of justice out onto the streets. I challenge the rulers of El Salvador to share their wealth, to stop the killings, to provide water, houses and schools for all … God is on the side of the poor. The Church sides with the poor.

3 Romero believed that the situation in El Salvador was unjust. But as a leader of the Roman Catholic Church he did not believe he should get involved in politics.

4 Then a close friend of Romero who had spoken out against the government was shot by the police.

5 Romero changed his mind. By not resisting the government he felt he was helping to prolong injustice. He became a leader of a powerful opposition movement.

7 On 21 March 1980 soldiers burst into Romero's Cathedral and gunned him down as he was celebrating the Eucharist.

This is my blood which is shed for you.

This is my body which is given up for you.

If they kill me, I want you to know that I now offer my blood to God for justice and the resurrection of El Salvador. I will rise again in the people of El Salvador.

6 He was threatened.

8 Romero's death became a symbol uniting many Christians together in their struggle to change El Salvador. A fair and democratic government was finally established in 1991.

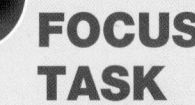

FOCUS TASK

'The Church's primary role must be a spiritual one. I say this as a member of the Anglican Church.'
Lord Jenkins of Roding, former Conservative MP

'You cannot apply the truth of God without being political.'
Roger Forster, evangelical Christian leader

1 Which speaker do you agree with more? Explain why.
2 How does a Christian decide what is unjust and what is simply unpopular?
3 'Religious believers have more responsibility than other people to protest against injustice in society.' Do you agree?
   Give reasons for your opinion, showing that you have thought about more than one point of view.

Is it ever right to fight?

Most Christians believe that war should be avoided. But there are many who also believe there are times when they might just have to fight, that there might be such a thing as a just war. In this investigation you will find out about these different attitudes to war, and you will test out one recent conflict to see if it really does qualify as a 'just war'.

✓ CHECKPOINT

Military service and the British army

Britain has a professional army. Everyone in it has joined by choice. The soldiers are paid a salary. This full-time army is supported by a part-time army called the Territorial Army which can be called on if needed.

The professional army has been involved in various conflicts in recent years. For more than 30 years soldiers have been serving in Northern Ireland. They have fought in two wars in the Middle East (see page 66). They have helped guard Britain against terrorist attack.

However, in comparison with many countries, Britain has been very peaceful since the Second World War. So soldiers often find themselves joining United Nations peace-keeping missions to areas which are recovering from past conflicts or helping the police and emergency services when there is a major disaster and sometimes (for instance during a firefighters' strike) doing the emergency services' work instead of them.

At various times in the past Britain has had a conscript army. During both World Wars all adult males had to sign up for military service. As recently as the 1960s all young men in Britain had to do a period of compulsory national service for two years.

If there were ever again to be a war involving Britain that needed more soldiers than the professional army could supply the government would have to get the agreement of Parliament to pass a bill to allow them to conscript people into the army.

⮕ STARTER

A

In the Image of Man by Robert Henderson Blyth, painted just after the Second World War (1939–45)

DISCUSS

Study Source A with a partner.

1 What has been damaged?
2 Why has it been damaged?
3 What is the attitude of the artist to the crucified Christ?
4 Why do you think it is called *In the Image of Man*?

KEY CHRISTIAN BELIEFS: War and peace

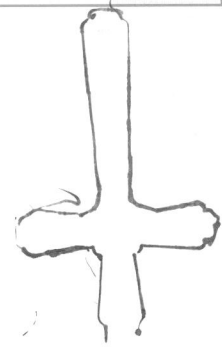

B

Jerusalem is the navel of the world. This royal city is now held captive by her enemies and is enslaved by a people which does not acknowledge God. She asks you to rescue her. All men going there who die, whether on the journey or while fighting the pagans will immediately be forgiven their sins. Until now you have fought and killed one another. Stop these hatreds amongst yourselves, silence the quarrels. Instead, rescue the Holy Land from that dreadful race.

Pope Urban's recruiting speech in 1095

1 Read Source B. How Christian do you think it is to say such things?

Most Christians believe that war should be avoided. But many also believe that there are times when a Christian may have to go to war. This is because they believe that the result of not going to war will be much worse.

The three main Christian stances towards war are shown in the diagram.

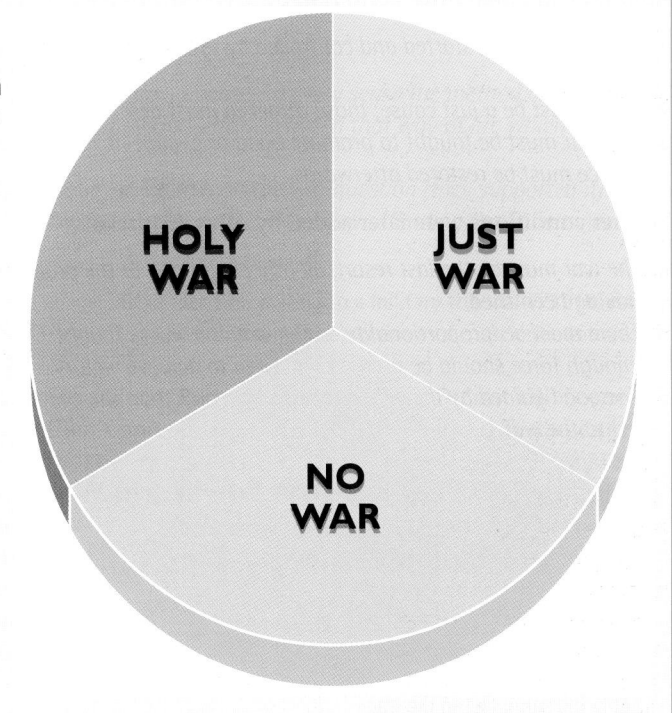

SAVE AS …

Make your own large copy of this diagram and use the information on the next five pages to add details to it. Include:

• what each idea means
• reasons used by Christians to support each idea
• an example of how this idea has been used in the past.

Holy war

Until the fourth century, Christian teaching was against the use of violence. Christians did not retaliate when persecuted, they did not join the army. However, all Christian teaching from this time about forgiveness, living at peace, not retaliating, is about the behaviour of individual Christians, not about national foreign policy.

As the Church became more politically powerful it faced a dilemma. The political leaders were Christians. Now they could affect the nation's foreign policy. Could the Church support a war?

There are examples in the Old Testament of God ordering war. For example, in 1 Samuel 15.2–3 God commands '[I will] punish the people of Amalek because their ancestors opposed the Israelites … Now go and attack the Amalekites and completely destroy everything they have.'

The idea developed of 'holy war' or war on behalf of God. The most famous examples of so-called holy war were the Christian wars to recover Jerusalem from the Muslims in the Middle Ages. Christians called them the Crusades, Muslims called them the Frankish invasions.

Whether the Church leaders who started the Crusades actually believed they were a holy war or just used that idea to win the support of the majority of ordinary Christians is not clear. Many of those fighting were certainly convinced that they were fighting a holy war on God's behalf.

The Crusades were a disaster. They soured relations between Western Europe and the Middle East to this day. They did not achieve any military objective. Terrible atrocities were committed in the name of God. Whole cities of people were slaughtered.

Some religions might have criteria for judging whether a war is a 'holy war' but nowadays there is no such idea in Christianity.

CASE STUDY: The Iraq War 2003

FOCUS TASK

Was it a just war?

In 2003 armies of the USA and Britain, supported by a few other nations, invaded Iraq. Did this war meet the criteria for a just war?
See what you think.

Question	Information	Just war – yes or no?
On whose authority?		
A just cause?		
To promote good or resist evil?		
A last resort?		
Only necessary force?		
Good gained? Peace & justice restored?		

1 Make your own copy of this table.

2 Using the information blocks below, makes notes in the second column. You will have to decide what belongs where.

3 In column 3 note whether the war meets each criterion. You should use your own judgement but you should also refer to Sources I–P.

The first stage of war was a massive bombing attack called Operation Shock and Awe. The Americans used technologically advanced computer-guided bombs (smart bombs) that could target individual buildings to try to avoid civilian casualties. Even so thousands of Iraqi civilians were killed or injured in the bombing. The next stage was a land invasion by ground troops. The Iraqi army quickly crumbled and this part of the war was over in a few weeks. Support for Saddam disappeared, his sons were killed and Saddam was captured alive.

The United Nations had tried various other means of solving the problem: sanctions, inspections and diplomacy. The Americans, with the support of the British, believed that all other means had been exhausted. Others disagreed and wanted to continue diplomatic efforts.

To start with the war was presented as if it was about weapons of mass destruction (WMD).
Saddam had resisted the inspectors and the Americans believed that he was developing weapons which could be launched on Britain at any moment. The purpose of the war changed once the decision had been made, particularly when they did not find WMD. Then it was justified as a campaign to get rid of a brutal dictator.

After the war Iraq collapsed into anarchy and chaos. Water supplies and electricity had been destroyed by the bombing. Hospitals were full to overflowing and doctors could not cope. There was looting and violence on the streets. There was no police force. Some of the most promising new leaders of Iraq were murdered by their opponents. The American and British troops, instead of helping to bring calm in Iraq, became themselves the victims of bomb attacks by extremist opponents of the invasion. The story is still continuing as we write …

The war was opposed by most members of the United Nations. Only Britain and America were prepared to send significant combat troops to fight in Iraq. The Americans and British however said they already had the authority of the United Nations because it had passed a resolution that allowed the UN to use all means necessary (including force if necessary) to remove Saddam Hussein's weapons of mass destruction (WMD) if he did not allow inspectors to do their work.

Saddam was a brutal dictator who caused immense suffering to his own people: gassing the Kurds; murdering people in cold blood; and invading his neighbour Kuwait. He also helped fund terrorism by paying $5000 to the families of any suicide bomber in Palestine. He diverted money that should have been going into humanitarian use in Iraq into paying for weapons and his own palaces.

Christian viewpoints on the Iraq war

I

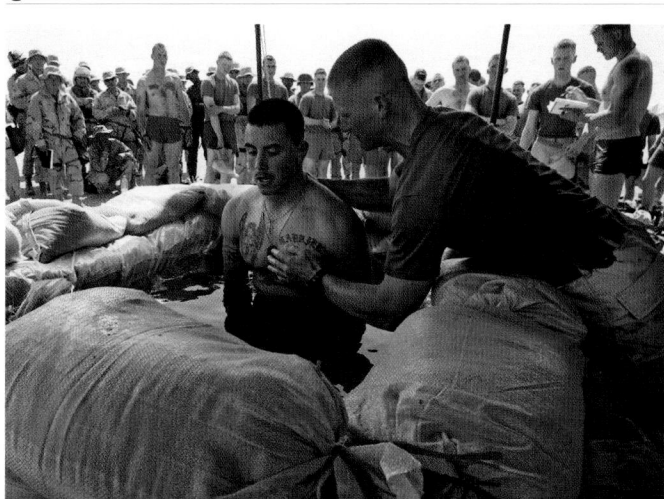

Clergy on a protest march against the war, 15 Feb 2003

J

Photo of American army chaplain baptising a soldier in the Iraqi desert in 2003

K

I believe that the war on Iraq is right. Saddam Hussein is an evil man, and we are right to use our armed forces to do anything in our power to remove him. I don't believe in the just war conditions some Christians use to decide whether to go to war – rather we need to be asking God directly what we should do.

Rosalind Barkly from London, in her 50s

L

The issue for the Church is whether we are following Jesus, not whether we are following the United Nations or the president of the United States. All powers and authorities are subject to Christ.

The DNA of a person who takes up a cross to follow Jesus ought to be coded for peace, not for war. In a time of war, Jesus would more likely be found on the front lines with medics and chaplains, helping soldiers and civilians who are hurt, than in the war room directing the bombing campaign.

Yet on the other hand the DNA of a cross-carrying Christian also ought to be coded for justice. Peace without justice is no peace at all and peace is not the absence of conflict. I fear we cannot find peace in this matter with Iraq by avoiding it.

The ideal is to follow Jesus' third way, which is to pursue alternative solutions to war without losing focus on the demands for both peace and justice.

Pastor George Mason of Wilshire Baptist Church in Dallas, Texas, USA

M

As time has passed, I have come to believe Saddam is a criminal who points weapons at people. If I have a weapon and he has a weapon and he has a history of using it, I'm probably not going to wait for him to shoot first. I see it as a just war in that sense. It is a pre-emptive strike, true. But because of the history ... This person is out of hand.

Baptist pastor Bob Campbell, Texas

N

Whether we agree with it or not, we're here. We just have to pray that God can still rule and control and protect even with war.

Baptist pastor John Ogletree, Texas

O

Violence isn't the answer to anything – war is morally and ethically wrong.

Catholic Sister Mary Ann Smith, of Ossining, New York, at an anti-war demonstration in 2003

P

Quaker Betty Hutchinson protests against the Iraq war in 2003

⊙ ISSUE: Violence v. non-violence in the struggle for liberation

Q

I thought that the Somoza government was so unjust that I had to join the resistance movement. As a Christian it was the only conclusion I could reach, but when I did so my Church could not understand why I was willing to fight and they expelled me.

Pablo, a young man in Nicaragua, read in the Bible that Jesus offered a just and fair life for all people. Most Nicaraguans did not have such a life so he decided to become an armed revolutionary.

As you saw on pages 60–61, many Christians have found themselves involved in struggles against injustice in their own country. Is taking up arms an acceptable option in these circumstances? Some Christians think so, as you can see from Sources Q–S.

Other Christians would argue that the only way to improve a bad situation is through non-violent action: marches, sit-ins, letters or demonstrations. For example, Oscar Romero (see page 61), despite being a victim of violence himself, always resisted those who thought Christians should join the armed struggle against their oppressors.

R

Jesus painted as a liberation fighter with a gun

S

One day it happened that a group of boys and girls from Solentiname, because of profound convictions and after having let it mature for a long time, decided to take up arms. Why did they do it? They did it for only one reason: their love for the kingdom of God, for the ardent desire that a just society be implanted, a real and concrete kingdom of God on Earth. When the time came, these boys and girls fought with great courage, but they also fought as Christians. That morning at San Carlos they tried several times with a loudspeaker to reason with the guardsmen so they might not have to fire a single shot. But the guardsmen responded to their reasoning with sub-machine-gun fire. With great regret they also were forced to shoot. Alejandro, one from my community, entered the building when in it there were no longer any but dead or wounded soldiers. He was going to set fire to it but, out of consideration for the wounded, he did not do it. I congratulate myself that these young Christians fought without hate – above all without hate for the wounded guardsmen, poor peasants like themselves, also exploited.

From a letter to the people of Nicaragua by the Catholic priest Ernesto Cardenal in December 1977. He was banned by his Church for supporting the revolutionaries, but after the success of the Revolution became a minister for education in the new government.

ACTIVITY

Imagine that Ernesto Cardenal (Source S) meets Martin Luther King. What might they say to each other about Christian attitudes to violence?

One of the most celebrated leaders of non-violent protest was Martin Luther King. You probably already know a good deal about him as he appears in many history and citizenship courses as well as religious studies.

T

Martin Luther King grew up in an intensely racist civilisation. In the 1950s, in the southern USA, black people were treated as second-class citizens. The blacks had separate universities, parks, cafes, toilets. Black schools had less money. Blacks were paid much less than whites for equally skilful jobs.

King was pastor of a Baptist church in Montgomery, Alabama. He saw the injustice of this situation. He devoted his life to the civil rights movement to change the laws that kept black people down.

Many believed that the best way to fight racism was with violence but King's faith led him to believe in non-violent protest. He believed that just as God had set the people of Israel free from slavery, he would liberate the black Americans from their oppression. But they had to do it Jesus' way. He used the words of Jesus, 'Love your enemies and pray for those who persecute you' as guidance through this fight for equality.

The first big protest he led was the Montgomery Bus Boycott. On the buses blacks and white were segregated. In protest blacks stopped using buses. Soon the bus companies could not carry on as their funds were running dry. They were losing 65 per cent of their fares without black custom. One year after the bus boycott, courts declared bus segregation illegal – which meant that other forms of segregation must also be illegal. Through non-violent direct action, blacks were on their way to equal civil rights.

There were many setbacks but King used the Bible to guide him through his fight for equality. He told protestors to pray for strength to remain non-violent. He got strength from the verse from the Sermon on the Mount, 'Happy are those who are persecuted'. Through the campaign King received death threats to himself and his family, two attempts to kill him; his home was firebombed and black leaders were attacked and imprisoned. King continued to preach the Christian principle: 'We must love our white brothers whatever they do'.

Eight years after the bus boycott, many from the civil rights movement marched to the state capital to demand voting rights. In the middle of the march the city police let dogs loose on the protestors, arresting 1000 including King, beating many with whips and clubs. Strengthened by King's Christian example the protestors still refused to retaliate. These images were then seen on TV across America. Many people were appalled at the images that exposed the viciousness of racism. King described racism as 'a boil or spot that had been hidden away for too long'. The scenes of brutal treatment by a racist police force had brought 'the ugliness of the boil to light'.

Martin Luther King achieved many great things. He was responsible for many of the early achievements of the civil rights movement and gave it the direction towards peaceful protests, which grew directly out of his Christian beliefs. In 1965 he won the Nobel Peace Prize and he continued to work for what he believed in up until he was killed in 1968.

ACTIVITY

Source T is a piece of GCSE coursework on Martin Luther King.

1 On your own copy:
  a) in one colour highlight examples of non-violent protest;
  b) in another colour highlight the religious principles on which non-violence was based;
  c) use your own research to add two more paragraphs giving other examples from the life and teachings of Martin Luther King.

DISCUSS

2 What do you think are the strengths and weaknesses of this piece of coursework?

Responsible stewards or plundering idiots?

How would you react if you lent a friend your favourite piece of clothing and they messed it up? Angry? Forgiving? That question may sound a million miles from religion and the environment but read on...we think there is a parallel. In this investigation you will explore **why** Christians believe they should look after the environment. At the end you will plan some targets to help them know **how** to do it.

✔ CHECKPOINT

Global warming
Burning fossil fuels such as oil produces carbon dioxide (CO_2). Most scientists believe this adds to the Greenhouse Effect, which causes global warming. This is bad news: it may cause ice caps to melt so low-lying areas around the world, including some of the most populated areas, will be flooded.

Deforestation
Forests act like a sponge, soaking up CO_2, so cutting down trees adds to the Greenhouse Effect. It also leads to desertification (good farming land turning to desert): once trees go, the soil gets eroded and loses its fertility.

Toxic waste
Industry and farming use chemicals that pollute rivers and oceans and damage ecosystems. Nuclear waste is a particular problem. It is deadly to all life for thousands of years after it is created. There is no safe way of disposing of it yet.

Renewable resources
Some resources are renewable: you can use them again and again. Forests are a renewable resource: new trees can be planted after mature ones are cut down. Other resources, such as oil, are non-renewable. Once you have used them up they are gone for ever. All the Earth's oil could be used up by 2050.

➲ STARTER

A

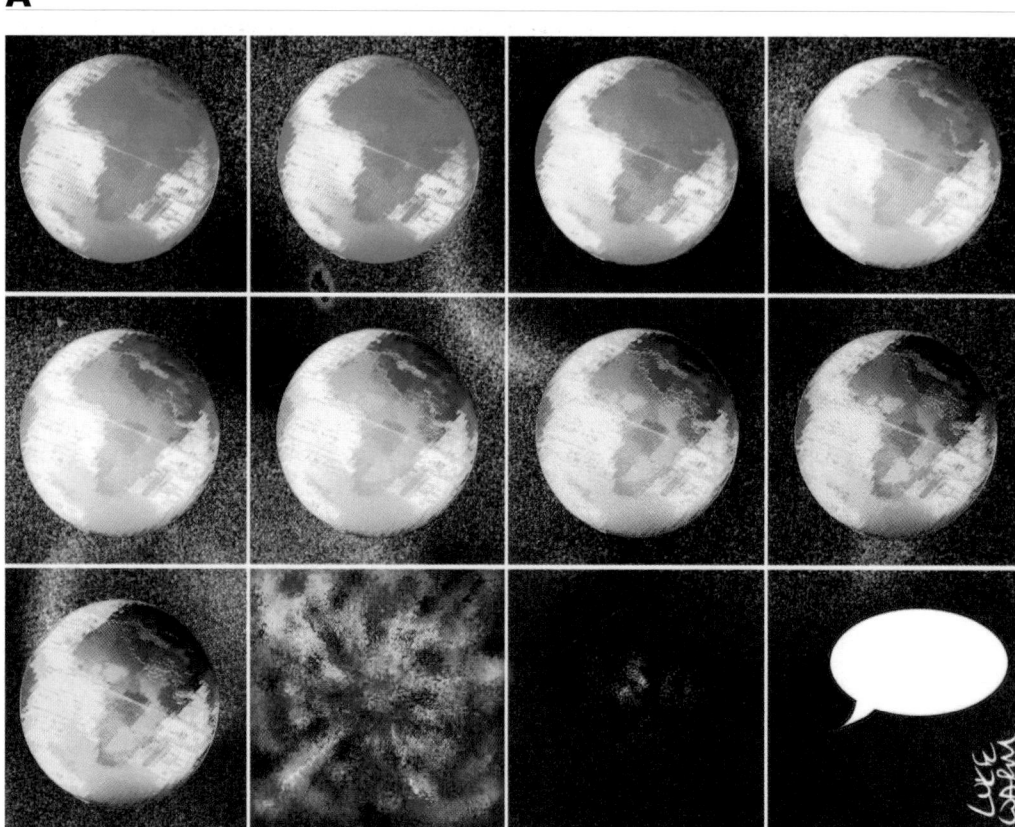

DISCUSS

1 We have blanked out the word bubble in the final frame. What do you think would be suitable words to go in it?
2 Your teacher can tell you what the original said. Then describe in your own words the message of this cartoon.

SAVE AS...

3 The checkpoint lists some ways that human beings are harming the environment.
   a) Using your own knowledge and research write some other bullet points to summarise at least two more examples.
   b) Divide the issues into two lists: the ones that you think you have power to do something about; and the ones that you think are beyond your control.

KEY CHRISTIAN BELIEFS: Christians and the environment

Christians believe that God created the world. Some Christians believe that God literally created the universe and the world in seven days – just as described in Genesis 1. Others believe that, while the world and human life were created by natural processes, these processes were still in the control of God. The world was created by the will of God. You will find out more about these two viewpoints on pages 82-83. For now we are more interested in how this belief affects Christian attitudes to the environment. There are three important ideas:

B

So God created human beings, making them to be like himself. He created them male and female, blessed them, and said, 'Have many children, so that your descendants will live all over the earth and bring it under their control. I am putting you in charge of the fish, the birds, and all the wild animals. I have provided all kinds of grain and all kinds of fruit for you to eat; but for all the wild animals and for all the birds I have provided grass and leafy plants for food' – and it was done. God saw all that he had made and it was very good … The Lord God placed the man in the garden of Eden to cultivate it and guard it.

Genesis 1.27–31, 2.15

Interdependence

Human beings are part of God's creation and all the different parts are linked together – with different plants and animals all created for a purpose within creation. So any damage to a part of creation is damaging to God and damaging to humanity as well.

Worship

When God had finished creation he admired it. Likewise humans should admire and celebrate creation and the God who created it. For many people the natural world with its wonders is the main thing that points them towards God and makes them want to worship. Celebrating the diversity and abundance of the creation is an important part of worship both for individual Christians and groups of Christians praying and singing about it, for example at harvest festivals. However, it is important to remember that Christians do not worship the creation itself (as some New Age religious groups do) but the God who created it.

Stewardship

According to the creation story human beings are given a special responsibility within creation: to cultivate it and guard it – to be 'good stewards'. A steward is someone who carefully looks after something that is not theirs, just like you'd expect a friend to look after anything you'd lent them. They look after it to the best of their ability for whoever really owns it – in this case, God. So it is the role of humans as stewards to pass on the world to the next generation in a better state than they received it.

C

1 *The Earth and all life on it is a gift from God given to us to share and develop, not to dominate and exploit.*

2 *Our actions have consequences for the rights of others and for the resources of the Earth.*

3 *The goods of the Earth and the beauties of nature are to be enjoyed and celebrated as well as consumed.*

4 *We have the responsibility to create a balanced policy between consumption and conservation.*

5 *We must consider the welfare of future generations in our planning for and utilisation of the Earth's resources.*

Pope John Paul II in *Sollicitudo Rei Socialis*, 1988, a publication by the Catholic Church on social justice and environmental issues

> ### DISCUSS
>
> Source C comes from the Catholic tradition but all Christian denominations tend to share similar views and have made similar pronouncements. Work with a partner to match each of the five points in Source C to one of the beliefs explained above. You could record your ideas in a table. Keep this as you will return to this source for the Focus Task on page 75.

Balancing rights and responsibilities

Some Christians have interpreted the creation story as giving people the right to exploit the environment. Most Christians would disagree, particularly now that they see the impact that human action is having on the environment. They would argue that in Genesis 1 and 2 rights are balanced against responsibilities. Later in the Bible, God gives very specific instructions about what we would now regard as responsible environmental stewardship, for example in Exodus 23.10–11 and Deuteronomy 20.19–20 (ensuring people don't over-farm the land or cut down trees). Some Christians are now among those taking a lead in helping people balance their environmental rights and responsibilities. They are taking a lead in protecting the environment.

D

Creator of Earth
and of all Earth's children,
Creator of soil and sea and sky
and the tapestries of stars,
we turn to you for guidance
as we look on our mutilated planet,
and pray it is not too late
for us to rescue our wounded world.
We have been so careless.
We have failed to nurture the fragile life
you entrusted to our keeping.
We beg you for forgiveness
and we ask you to begin again.
Be with us in our commitment to Earth.
Let all the Earth say: Amen.

A prayer by Miriam Therese Winter, from the
SPCK Book of Christian Prayer

DISCUSS

1 How significant do you think the activities in Source E are as examples of environmental action?
2 In your class, brainstorm the rights and responsibilities that people have for their environment. Record them in a table like the one below. Can you think of any more rights? Try to think of at least one responsibility to go with each right.
3 In the third column, give an example of a practical action a Christian could take to fulfil this responsibility.

Environmental rights	Environmental responsibilities	Action
A beautiful world to live in	Keep nature clean and tidy	
Food to eat		
Shelter		
Water to drink		
Clean air to breathe		

E

Top: outdoor service at Coventry Cathedral following the launch of Operation Noah, a campaign by Christian churches to curb human-induced climate change; bottom: a 'subverted' advertisement commenting on traffic pollution

CASE STUDY: Bonsall . . .

. . . environmental celebration

A well dressing at Bonsall: this picture made of flowers will be placed on a well.

'Nobody is sure how well-dressing began. Some like to think it dates back to the times of the Great Plague in England. Then pure, clean water was literally a gift of life! Others say that the Celts and the Ancient Greeks used to decorate water springs with flowers as a sign of respect to the gods.'

'Nowadays we like to dress wells because it's a bit of fun. But also it gives us a chance to worship God as the Creator of the world. We give thanks for the water that sustains our lives and the beautiful flowers and trees in our gardens.'

'All the wells in the village are blessed by the local vicar in a special Sunday service. We sing hymns and say a prayer at each well. At some we listen to a reading from the Bible. We also try to collect money from visitors. This goes to support a charity, often connected with children.'

. . . environmental action

Bonsall is on the edge of the Peak District National Park and is designated as a conservation area by Derbyshire County Council.

Ken Edgar is a father and grandfather who is committed to looking after the environment for future generations. He is an Anglican who was a church warden in the village church. He has also served on Bonsall Parish Council.

> The main threats to our environment are from acid rain, transport and quarrying.
> Even the well-dressings have been affected by damage to the environment. We used to use black moss for the background but it is slow-growing, and in recent years it has been attacked by acid rain so now there is a preservation order on it and we have to use other natural materials.
> The parish council tries to listen to people's concerns and act on them. For example, we were worried about the number of lorries parked on narrow roads in the village, so everyone in the village worked together to develop Church land into a lorry park with a children's play area by the side of it. This has been a great success.

> I am worried, however, about the damage which is being done to the moors above the village. The rock contains valuable limestone and fluorspar. Firms are keen to extract it but do not meet their promises to reclaim the land afterwards. I think too many people are greedy and only worried about their own interests.
> The parish church has little real power over issues like this. We can comment on local planning applications if we think that the environment is in danger, but in the end we can't really stop anyone.

ACTIVITY

1 In groups, imagine you are helping to plan next year's well-dressing in Bonsall. The theme is 'Christian care for the environment' and you have been asked to make a display for one of the wells. You need to choose a passage from the Bible or a key belief and plan a well-dressing panel to reflect that theme. Your display could also refer to some of the action that people in Bonsall have taken in the past to care for their environment.

SAVE AS ...

2 Do the Christians in Bonsall have more responsibility than the other villagers to look after the environment? Write two paragraphs. Give more than one point of view to explain your answer.

Can you prove that God exists?

There are many reasons to believe that God exists and many reasons not to. You are now going to look at some of the reasons in greater detail and see how well they stand up when challenged.

FOCUS TASK

You will look at three arguments.

1 Where did the universe come from?
2 Did life on Earth happen by design or by chance?
3 Is religious experience real or illusory?

As you work through the unit add details to a diagram like this and use it to write a carefully balanced philosophical essay.

Argument 1: Origins of the universe – the cosmological argument

> Where else could the universe come from?

A common argument for believing in God is that the universe must have come from somewhere. Christians believe it came from God.

An early version of this belief is the Creation story in the Bible. In Chapters 1 and 2 of Genesis God creates the universe and everything in it out of nothing.

Philosophers since then have developed this 'cosmological' argument in various ways.

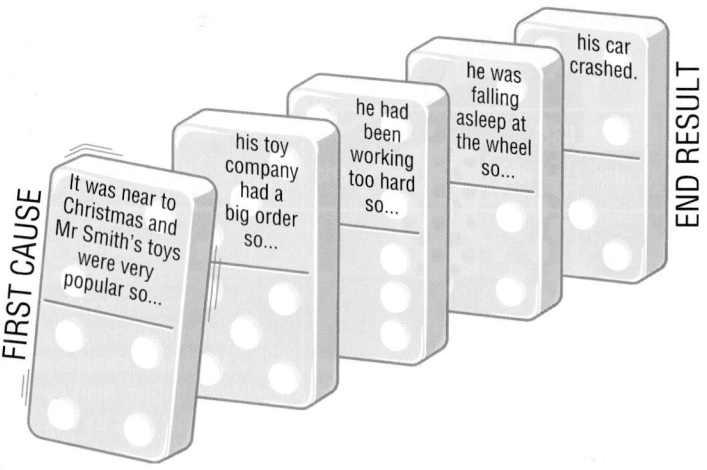

Aquinas and the First Cause

Thomas Aquinas was one of the leading scholars of the Middle Ages. Seven hundred years ago he devised several arguments for the existence of God. One of his arguments was the 'First Cause' argument. He argued that everything in the universe has a cause. Whatever happens in the universe can be traced back through a whole series of causes to some first event that made the rest happen. An example from modern life would be to explain a car crash.

Just as the first domino in a row must be toppled, so the first event must happen to set off the chain reaction. That is the first cause. Aquinas said that everything in the universe can be traced back to a First Cause. That First Cause is God, Himself an uncaused 'necessary' being.

Recent discoveries in science have given the First Cause argument new life.

The theory of the Big Bang is that once, all matter in the universe was concentrated into an incredibly dense mass. It was much smaller than the eye of a needle. For some reason, 15,000 million years ago it began to expand.

This expansion is called 'The Big Bang' although this term was originally used by the theory's critics to ridicule it! A better image might be 'The Big Bloom', as the opening out of the universe was orderly, like a flower blooming, although with the speed and force of an explosion.

From that point, the universe has continued its rapid expansion to this day, and our Earth, like all the planets, stars and matter in the universe, comes from the cooling and gathering of matter sent out by the Big Bang. The universe will one day stop expanding and start contracting.

One alternative theory – the Steady State theory – says that the universe is not changing and had no beginning, and that therefore the Big Bang is nonsense. However, few scientists today accept the Steady State theory.

What caused the Big Bang?

The Big Bang theory is widely accepted by people today – including many Christians – even though there are unanswered and currently unanswerable questions about it. You can probably see the attraction of the theory to some Christians. From the religious point of view the most important unanswered question is what triggered the Big Bang.

Chance?

Some say it was pure chance; that in the particular unusual conditions that prevailed 15,000 million years ago, what we now recognise as the laws of cause and effect did not apply. No one was needed to cause the expansion of the universe. This is an explanation favoured by atheists and agnostics.

God?

An alternative view is that it was an act of God which, in some way, triggered the Big Bang. This position is favoured by theists. In Aquinas' terms, God was the First Cause that triggered the Big Bang.

A

Most people believe that God allows the universe to evolve according to a set of laws and does not intervene to break those laws ... but it would still be up to God to wind up the clockwork and choose how to start it off. So long as the universe had a beginning, we could suppose it had a Creator.

From *A Brief History of Time* by Professor Stephen Hawking, 1988

B

For the scientist who has lived by his faith in the power of reason, the story ends like a bad dream. He has scaled the mountains of ignorance; he is about to conquer the highest peak; and as he pulls himself over the final rock, he is greeted by a band of theologians who have been sitting there for centuries!

Robert Jastrow, American Christian astrophysicist

DISCUSS

1 What point is being made in Source B?
2 Which explanation of the Big Bang do you favour:
   a) that it was caused by chance, or
   b) that it was caused by God, or
   c) that it never happened?
   Explain your view, showing that you have considered an alternative viewpoint.

SAVE AS ...

3 Write your own 'postcard-sized' summaries of:
   a) The cosmological argument
   b) The Big Bang theory.

Argument 2: The design of the natural world – the teleological argument

> Such an intricate world must have been designed by someone.

A second common argument Christians give for God's existence is that the world around them shows a pattern and therefore it must have been created or designed by someone. This is known as the argument of 'design' – the belief that everything in the human body and the natural world is so intricately designed that this could not have happened by random chance.

Two famous Christians in history based their 'design' arguments around a thumb and a watch.

ACTIVITY

Choose one of the pictures below and, before reading the material opposite, see if you can think how someone might use it to argue that God exists.

SAVE AS ...

Make sure you have recorded the arguments of both Newton and Paley on your copy of the table on page 77, using their examples or your own.

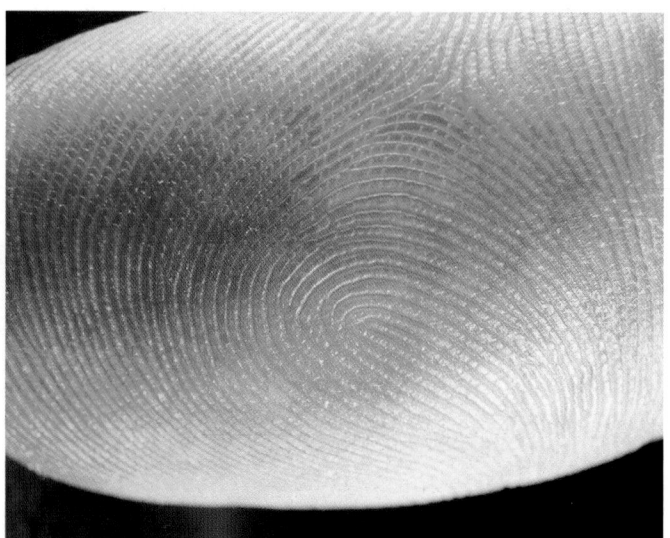

Newton and the thumb

Sir Isaac Newton, 1642–1727, one of the founders of modern science, said: 'In the absence of any other proof, the thumb alone would convince me of God's existence.' Newton believed that such intricate designs as the human thumb, unique to each individual, must have had a designer.

Paley and the watch

One hundred years after Newton, William Paley (1743–1805), a philosopher, used a watch to explain why he believed in God. Paley's argument was more complicated than Newton's. He compared the watch to the world. In the 18th century a watch was one of the most intricate pieces of machinery made by human beings.

Paley argued that if he were to find a watch lying on the ground, he would assume that it was the product of a designer for, unlike a stone, he would see at once that it was made up of many different parts which worked together to produce movement. If any one of these parts was ordered slightly differently then the whole structure would not work. Paley argued that, in the same way, the world is like a machine, and if the world is like a machine, it must have a designer. Paley concluded that this designer is God.

Nietzsche and an imperfect world

There are problems with both Newton's and Paley's arguments. The 19th-century German philosopher Friedrich Nietzsche completely disagreed with them. He argued that God was 'dead'!

Nietzsche refused to see order in the world. Take, for example, the way the Earth's crust is made up of plates which do not fit together precisely. This causes tremors, volcanoes and earthquakes. 'How could a God who is good create a world so imperfect?' argued Nietzsche.

Nietzsche concluded that there was no God, there were no natural laws, and there was no order. Scientists had made incorrect observations about the world and had invented laws based on these. Nietzsche believed that there is no absolute truth about the world and no ultimate purpose, a view known as 'nihilism'. You will return to this 'problem' with belief in God on page 102.

DISCUSS

Ancient Greek philosophers used to discuss problems like the existence of God in the street or over drinks.

In an imaginary café (which does not exist in regular time) Paley meets Nietzsche, Darwin or Dawkins. What do you think they might say to each other over coffee?

ACTIVITY

'If God designed the world, I think that he should be sacked.'

1 Explain in your own words what the speaker means.
2 Explain whether you agree or disagree with this statement. Support your answer with reference to material from pages 80 and 81. Show that you have considered another viewpoint.

Darwin and natural selection

A scientific challenge to the design argument came from the theory of evolution (see page 82). In the 19th century Charles Darwin (1809–82) developed his theory that all life evolves by natural selection. For example, on an island where the main food supply is hard nuts, only the finches with excellent nut-cracking beaks survive to breed more strong-beaked finches. The animals or plants that are best suited to their environment survive. Those that are not die out. According to this theory, human, animal and plant life had designed itself! However, Darwin never attempted to explain where the original building blocks of life on Earth came from, just how they adapted and changed once they were here.

Intelligent design

In response to Darwin's theory, some Christians put forward the theory of intelligent design. Evolution might explain the process by which the natural world as we know it has been created but the process does not seem random to them. They see evidence of an 'intelligence' driving forward those changes to create ever more complex organisms such as the human eye or DNA. However, this argument has weaknesses too.

C

To explain the origin of the DNA/protein machine by invoking a supernatural Designer is to explain precisely nothing, for it leaves unexplained the origin of the Designer. You have to say something like 'God was always there', and if you allow yourself that kind of lazy way out, you might as well just say 'DNA was always there', or 'Life was always there', and be done with it.

Richard Dawkins, *The Blind Watchmaker: Why the Evidence of Evolution Reveals a Universe without Design*

How do Christians interpret Genesis 1 and 2?

DISCUSS

1 Find the Creation story in Genesis 1 and read the full account of each stage shown in Source D.
2 What does this account suggest about:
   a) God
   b) the world
   c) human beings?
3 How might Genesis 1 and 2 give meaning, value or purpose to a Christian's life?

Let's briefly step aside from exploring arguments for the existence of God and look in more detail at the relationship of religion and science, and specifically the apparent conflict between creation and evolution.

To many Christians the Big Bang and evolution seem plausible explanations for the origins of the universe and of life on Earth. Yet they differ in many details from the creation stories in Genesis 1 and 2.

How does this affect the way Christians read the Creation stories at the beginning of the Bible?

D

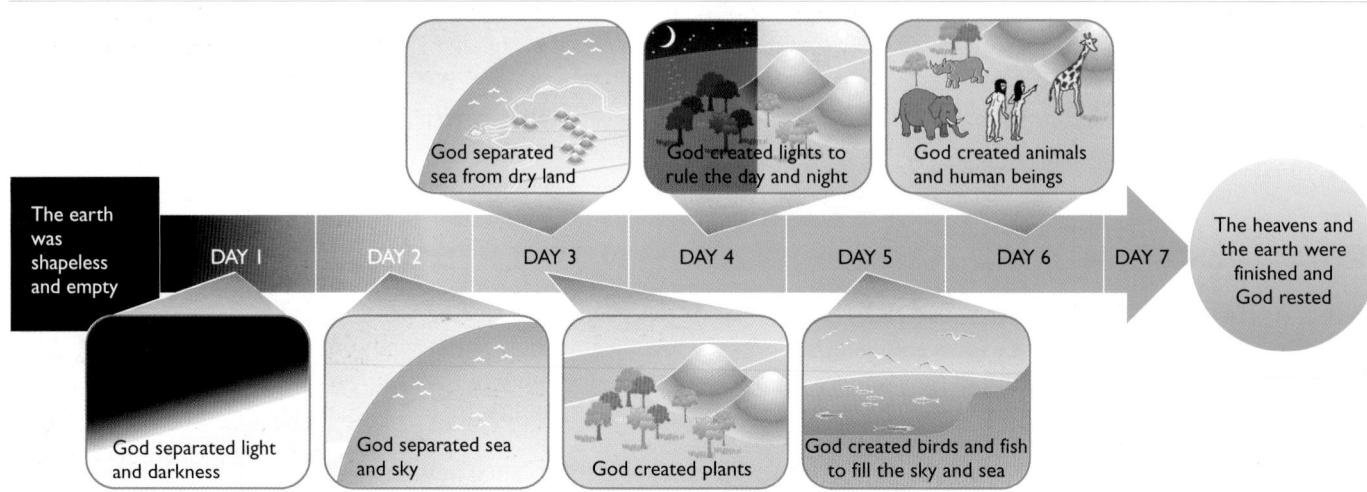

The stages of Creation according to the Bible

'Creation' according to Darwin

In past centuries many people believed the Bible's account of Creation to be literally true. In the 17th century Archbishop Ussher even calculated the exact time when God finally finished Creation (9 a.m. on Friday 23 October, 4004 BCE).

With the development of scientific thinking in the 19th century, and particularly the theory of evolution, three aspects of the Bible Creation story were questioned.

E

Time scale
❏ The process science was describing took many **hundreds of millions of years**.
❏ The process according to the Bible took **six days**.

Process
❏ Darwin's 'natural selection' was **unguided**. There were no rights and wrongs, just the strong and the weak – the world had designed itself through the survival of the fittest.
❏ The Bible in contrast shows **God very firmly in charge**.

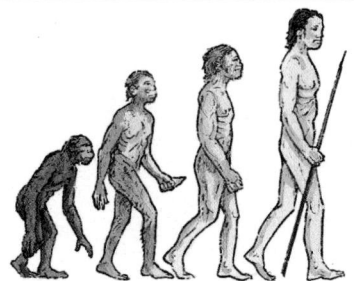

The place of human life
❏ Evolution had human beings **evolving from apes**.
❏ The Bible, by contrast, had humans made **'in God's image'** on the sixth day of Creation.

What kind of truth is Genesis 1 and 2?

Some Christians found Darwin's theory a threat to their faith, because it appeared to challenge the authority of the Bible. If the Bible was wrong on this, might it be wrong on other things too? They preferred to maintain a 'literalist' reading of Genesis 1 and 2 (see Source G). This viewpoint is known as Creationism. Creationists have succeeded in banning the teaching of the theory of evolution in some states in the USA.

However, other Christians see no contradiction between Genesis 1 and 2 and scientific theories such as evolution. They see no conflict generally between science and religion. Many scientists are Christian believers. These Christians say that science and religion are asking different questions.

When they consider the Bible, these Christians do not look for scientific truth. What they expect the Bible to give them is the truth about God and God's relationship with human beings. They see natural selection as a plausible, if unproved, explanation for life on Earth. They take a 'relativist' attitude to the Bible. They don't read Genesis 1 and 2 as literally true but they still see it as an authoritative account of God's relationship with human beings and other living creatures. It tells them that all life on Earth is part of God's plan and that humans are special with special rights and responsibilities.

F

Science asks **how** *things have happened, religion asks* **why**. *Genesis is not there to give short, technical answers about how the universe began. It gives us the big answer that things exist because of God's will. One can perfectly well believe in the Big Bang, but believe in it as well as the will of God the creator.*

John Polkinghorne, a Christian and a scientist at Cambridge University

H

The Bible contains many different kinds of literature: poems, proverbs, history, letters, allegories, parables, etc. The first task in reading the creation stories is to decide what kind of writing this is. Genesis 1 and 2 bears all the marks of being a poem, or a hymn, or a teaching to be used in worship. Such poetry has the strength of conveying powerful ideas about God, but all the limitations in scientific understanding that you would expect of a writer of many thousands of years ago limited to their own scientific knowledge.

Dr David Wilkinson, an astrophysicist

G

I don't believe evolution is true. I believe Creation is true: that God created the world in six, 24-hour days. If there is a God, he can do anything. If God created by evolution, it doesn't give him half the glory it would if he created the world from scratch. Scientific knowledge is human knowledge. I prefer to trust God's truth because he has been there from the beginning.

Astrid, a London student, explains why she wears this tee-shirt saying 'Our Father?! Evolution: the wisdom of men is foolishness to God (1 Corinthians 1.20)'.

ACTIVITY

1 Look at Source G. Create a design for a tee-shirt that sums up what **you** believe about creation and evolution.

DISCUSS

2 Is it possible for Christians to believe in the Bible creation story **and** the theory of evolution? Discuss your response with a partner and list the problems each view raises for Christians.

Argument 3: Religious experience

> I know God exists.
> Who else healed me?

A third argument for the existence of God is religious experience. People meet God. They feel God. They hear God. Or they say they do! For them, their experience is the ultimate proof. But is it enough to convince others?

Was John Rajah healed by God?

In 1987 John Rajah, an insurance worker, developed stomach pains. In the summer of 1988 his condition rapidly worsened.

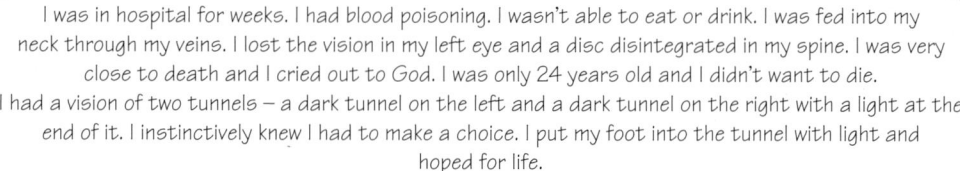

> I was in hospital for weeks. I had blood poisoning. I wasn't able to eat or drink. I was fed into my neck through my veins. I lost the vision in my left eye and a disc disintegrated in my spine. I was very close to death and I cried out to God. I was only 24 years old and I didn't want to die.
> I had a vision of two tunnels – a dark tunnel on the left and a dark tunnel on the right with a light at the end of it. I instinctively knew I had to make a choice. I put my foot into the tunnel with light and hoped for life.
> After that experience I decided to seek God.

The doctors did not know what caused John's disease, which was a form of colitis. Surgery was a last resort. His colon was removed. He had a colostomy bag instead. He wore a surgical corset, to support his spine. He was in constant pain and walked hunched over like an old man.

In summer 1990 John went to Holy Trinity, Brompton, an Evangelical Anglican church. At the end of the service, the vicar invited people to come forward for prayer. John felt at peace and went forward. He made a commitment to follow Jesus.

> I followed up my commitment to God by joining an 'Alpha course' at my church (an Alpha Course is an introduction to Christianity, commonly used in evangelical churches). On 18 March 1992 the talk was on healing and the team began to pray for the sick. Two people said they felt there was someone present with problems regarding their colon and God wanted to heal them. The leader asked that if anyone was present with the disease colitis they come forward for prayer. I thought, 'This has got to be me!'
> They prayed for me.
> At the time I did not feel any different. But I went home and decided I was going to have faith that God had healed me. I decided to put aside all my medication and, trusting completely in God's word, prayed in hope.
> When I woke up the next day there was no pain and I wasn't bleeding! I was unsure of what was going on and for a while I was scared but realised God had touched me. From that day on, I became fitter and stronger and no longer depended on tablets. It was amazing – Jesus healed me and set me free. The effects of surgery and its consequences from the years of illness are still present but I am not daunted because God has healed me, is still healing me and will continue to heal me.

> I am John's sister. I am a doctor. At the time of John's medical problems I was not a Christian, but through seeing him miraculously get better and hearing his account of his cure, I came to believe in the possibility that God had healed him. I went on an Alpha course to find out more and, through John's healing, I too am now a Christian.

> It is now June 2004 and there is no disease present since the moment God touched and healed me all those years ago on the Alpha course. I am so very grateful to Him for what He has done in and with my life. I have recently given up my job at the bank to work full time for God, helping children who are in need and at risk around the world.

DISCUSS

Explain the role of each of the following in John Rajah's healing:

- a vision
- prayer
- other Christians
- John's own actions
- miraculous intervention by God.

When people read a story like John Rajah's, they tend to find evidence to support their existing ideas. If they do believe that God can heal someone in this way then they find evidence to support their belief. If not, then they find evidence to confirm their doubt.

The believer might say that the doubter's spiritual awareness is underdeveloped so they cannot see God at work. The sceptic will say that the believer's spiritual awareness is overdeveloped so they see God in things that have a rational explanation.

✔ CHECKPOINT

Other forms of experience

If you use this as a case study in your exam, you may need to classify it: John Rajah had a vision; he experienced prayer and people praying for him; those prayers were answered; and there was a miracle.

John Rajah's is only one sort of experience. On pages 98–99 you will study other forms of religious experience. You will need to think about whether such experiences are more or less convincing evidence of the existence of God than the story of John Rajah.

ROLE PLAY

1 Work in pairs and take one role each – a believer and a doubter. The believer should argue that John Rajah's experience proves the existence of God, the doubter should argue that his experience has other explanations.
2 Swap roles and repeat the exercise.
3 In your own words, explain the difficulties facing someone:
   a) trying to disprove someone else's experience of God
   b) trying to prove their own experience of God.

🔍 FOCUS TASK

Work in groups.

1 Make a large simplified copy of the diagram below on an A3 piece of paper.

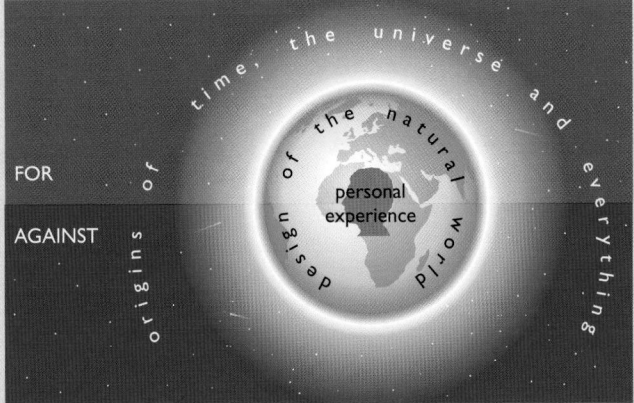

2 Write each of the statements on the right on a separate slip of paper.
3 Place each statement where you think it best fits on your diagram. Try to agree the positions with the rest of the group.
4 Once you have agreed all the positions, paste the statements onto the diagram.

On your own

5 You are now ready to write up your findings in an essay about arguments for and against the existence of God. Write a paragraph on each argument, making sure you have summarised both why some people accept it and why other people reject it. Conclude with your own view as to whether God exists, explaining why you believe this but showing that you have considered other points of view.

> Religious experience is all in the mind.

> There is a God-given order in the natural world.

> There is cruelty and suffering in the natural world.

> God is the First Cause of the universe.

> God has answered my prayers.

> The Big Bang happened by chance.

What is God like?

Most people have an image of God, even if it is simply an image of something they do not believe in! In this investigation you will consider different images of God, comparing them with your own. For your final task you will write an essay.

➡ STARTER

A class of students in a Christian school in England were asked to draw their ideas about God. Sources A and B show two of their drawings.

B

A

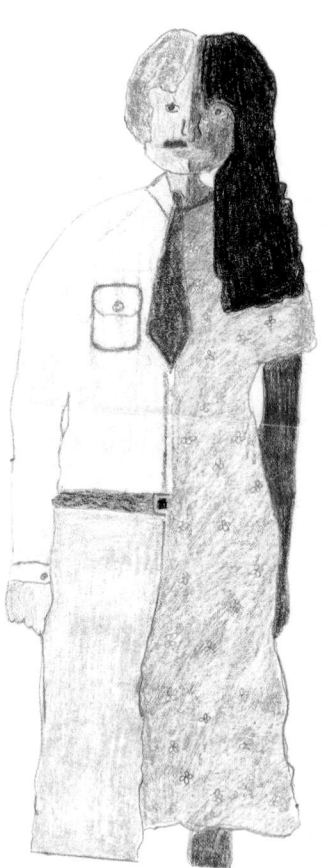

ACTIVITY

1 Look carefully at Sources A–D.
2 Choose the idea that is nearest to your own image of God. Write down three reasons why you chose it. If none of them is near, go straight to Question 3.
3 Choose the idea that is furthest away from your image of God. Write down three reasons why you chose that one.

Sources C and D show images from Christian churches in England and Germany.

C

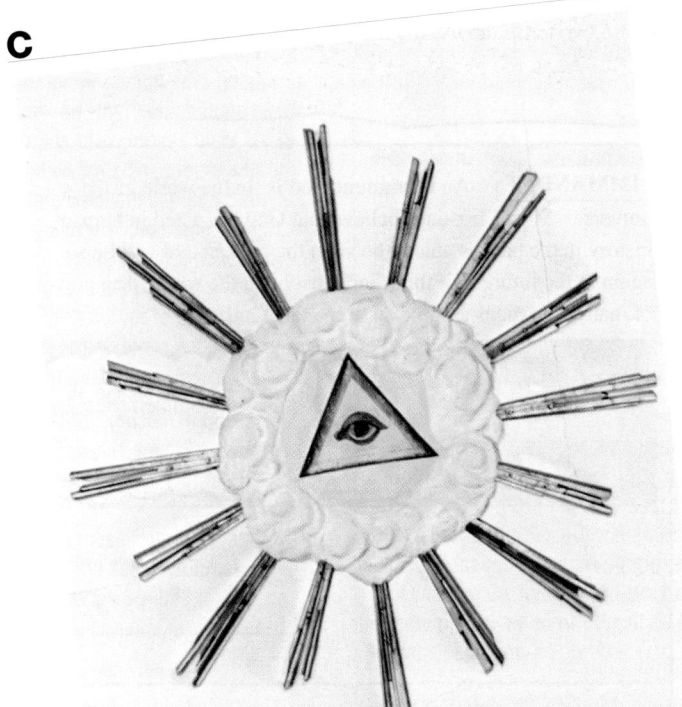

D

E

> If triangles had a god, he would have three sides.

Montesquieu, 1721

> The god of the cannibal will be a cannibal, of the crusaders a crusader, of the merchant, a merchant.

Emerson, 1860

> God is what man finds that is divine in himself. God is the best way man can behave in the ordinary occasions of life and the farthest point to which man can stretch himself.

Max Lerner, 1959

It is impossible to convey either in pictures or words what God is really like, because God is beyond human understanding. When people talk about God they therefore use pictures or concrete images or symbolic language to convey some selected quality of God. They sometimes use human images – e.g. calling God a shepherd or a king – this is known as 'anthropomorphism'. These human images help others to picture God, but at the same time they limit God. God is not a human being. God is not male or female. God is not an eye. God does not have eyes!

The Bible uses many images to symbolise God's presence – fire, a dove, but God is not a fire and not a bird!

You will need to keep this idea in mind over the next six pages as you examine various Christian ideas about God. Thinking and writing about God is interesting, but also open to misunderstanding, so it requires a lot of patience!

DISCUSS

1 Do you think the people who created Sources A–D believe this is what God actually looks like? Explain your answer.
2 What point are the speakers in Source E making?
3 Many religions forbid drawings or images of God. The second of the Ten Commandments forbids it. Why do you think this is? Exodus 20.4 may help you.

The Trinity

Most Christians believe that God has three persons, which they call Father, Son and Holy Spirit.

K

The Father – the transcendent – 'God beyond us' who created the world and keeps it going.

Jesus, the Son – the immanent and personal – 'God beside us' who came to earth and lived a human life.

God the Father, *God beyond us, we adore you.*
You are the depth of all that is.
You are the ground of our being.
We can never grasp you, yet you grasp us;
the universe speaks of you to us, and your love
comes to us through Jesus.

God the Son, *God beside us, we adore you.*
You are the perfection of humanity.
You have shown us what human life should be like.
In you we see divine love and human greatness
combined.

God the Spirit, *God around us, we adore you.*
You draw us to Jesus and the Father.
You are power within us.
You give us abundant life and can make us
the men and women we are meant to be.

Father, Son, and Spirit;
God, beyond, beside and around us;
We adore you.

A prayer for Trinity Sunday by
Caryl Micklem, from
Contemporary Prayers

The Spirit – the immanent yet impersonal – 'God around us' who inspires and guides Christians from day to day.

L

… Jesus came from Nazareth in the province of Galilee, and was baptized by John in the Jordan. As soon as Jesus came up out of the water, he saw heaven opening and the Spirit coming down on him like a dove. And a voice came from heaven, 'You are my own dear Son. I am pleased with you.'

An account of Jesus' baptism
(Mark 1.9–11)

SAVE AS …

1 Study carefully what Source K is saying about:
  a) the Father
  b) the Son
  c) the Spirit.
2 Record the characteristics of each person of the Trinity on your grid from page 89.

ACTIVITY

1 Working with a partner discuss how the artists who made Sources M and N have tried to show the Trinity. In your discussions focus on the use of shape, colour, symbols, words and space.
2 Which do you think is the more successful representation?
3 Choose one image and write a 100-word summary of the Christian idea of the Trinity which could be displayed alongside the image in an exhibition of Christian art.

✔ CHECKPOINT

One God or many?
Monotheism is believing in one God. **Polytheism** is believing in more than one god. Over the centuries Christian belief in the Trinity has caused much confusion. Critics say that Christians really believe in three gods. Christians say not.

> Why don't you come clean and admit that Christians believe in three gods?

> Because we don't! Christianity is a monotheistic religion, just like Islam and Judaism.

> Well how do you explain 'the Trinity' – God the Father, God the Son and God the Holy Spirit'?

> Trinity doesn't mean three gods, but one God in three persons. It makes better sense if you say 'God who is Father, Son and Holy Spirit'.

> So is it really just three aspects of God?

> Not exactly! Some Christians explain it like this: a person can be mother, sister and daughter at the same time. These are different relationships and roles, but the same person. Others compare the Trinity to ice, water and steam – the same substance in three forms. Others would say both those comparisons are quite misleading. That there is one God, but known in three persons.

M

Part of a wallpainting showing the Trinity by Masaccio, painted in 1427–8

N

A modern painting of the Trinity by John Piper, in Chichester Cathedral. The Trinity is shown in the three central panels.

Jesus

Jesus Christ is at the centre of Christian faith. The term 'Christian' means 'follower of Christ'. Let's examine a few of the basic beliefs that Christians have about Jesus.

Jesus is both fully God and fully human

Christians who believe in the Trinity believe that Jesus was God in a human body. They use the word 'incarnation' to describe this. Incarnation means becoming flesh. The festival of Christmas is a celebration of the **incarnation** – of God coming to Earth as a person.

The incarnation is deeply significant to Christians because it shows that God takes an active role in the lives of people. God becomes accessible and approachable, i.e. immanent and personal. In Jesus, God lived a totally human **life**. One of Jesus' other names is Immanuel, which means 'God with us.' In Jesus, God was most immanent: in the world, a part of the world, yet influencing it.

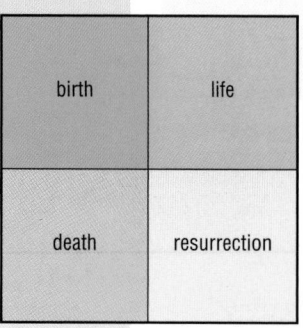

Jesus' teachings guide Christians in their daily lives

Jesus Christ is the perfect example of God-like attitudes and behaviour. Jesus' sermons, parables, miracles and actions show Christians how they should live.

Jesus' death resolves the problem of sin

If Jesus was God in human form then his **death** also has particular importance. God is eternal, so God cannot die. So why did Jesus die? One common Christian explanation is that Jesus' death was part of God's plan for removing sin. All people fall short of God's standards; the fair punishment for this would be death. However, Jesus, who was both God and the only truly sinless human who ever lived, has taken the punishment on behalf of all people. God's forgiveness is, therefore, available to anyone. This is what Christians mean when they say that Christ is the 'Redeemer' or 'Saviour' of the world.

Jesus' resurrection resolves the problem of death

Jesus did not stay dead. He **rose from death** and returned to his Father for eternity. The same gift of eternal life is available to his followers (see page 111).

O

I believe in Jesus Christ, [God's] only Son, our Lord.
He was conceived by the power of the Holy Spirit
and born of the Virgin Mary.
He suffered under Pontius Pilate, was crucified, died, and was buried.
He descended to the dead.
On the third day he rose again.
He ascended into heaven,
and is seated at the right hand of the Father.
He will come again to judge the living and the dead.

Part of the *Apostles' Creed*

ACTIVITY

Every time Christians say the Apostles' Creed (Source O) they restate their most basic beliefs about Jesus.

1 Draw up a table like the one below.

Jesus as a human being	Jesus as God
He was born to a human mother	His mother was a virgin

2 Look at Source O. Write each claim about Jesus in the appropriate column.
3 How do you think a creed like this, written more than 1500 years ago, is useful to Christians today?

SAVE AS ...

4 Record in your own words what the word 'incarnation' means, and why it is important to Christians.

P

Femme Touchant Jesus (*Woman touching Jesus*)
by Corinne Vonaesch, 2001

Q

Christ expels the money-changers from the temple by Edward Burra

DISCUSS

1 Sources P and Q show two stories from the Gospels. One is Matthew 9.20–22, the other is Matthew 21.12–13. Look up the passages in a Bible and decide which story goes with which picture.
2 Compare the way the two pictures portray Jesus. What are the similarities and differences in the way Jesus is presented?
3 Look back to the pictures of Jesus on pages 48–49. Taking all these pictures, which is the closest to the way *you* picture Jesus? Explain your choice.

ACTIVITY

4 Imagine you have to make a six-frame story strip of Jesus' life for someone who knows almost nothing about it. Using your own research or background knowledge and the information on page 92 decide what your six frames ought to show. What aspects of Jesus will you focus on? If you want help starting out you could look up these references. All are from Matthew's Gospel:

1.18–25 (the birth of Jesus)
5.1–11 (the Sermon on the Mount)
14.13–33 (the feeding of the 5000 and walking on water)
26.26–30 (the Last Supper)
27.32–50 (the Crucifixion)
28.1–10 (the Resurrection)

FOCUS TASK

'A God we can understand is no God at all.'
This was said by St John Chrysostom 1600 years ago. Do you agree with what St John said?
   Write an essay that explores this question. Make use of all the material you have read on pages 86–93.

6.4 One God, revealed in many ways

HOW IS GOD REVEALED?

If you want to get to know someone what do you do? You write to them or arrange to meet them. If you want to get to know God what do you do? That is what this investigation is all about. You have already come across many of the main ideas so the first spread is just a recap and the second gives you two contrasting case studies. Then it is over to you to draw a concept map summing up the types of Christian revelation.

DISCUSS

Read Source A. Do you agree it would be fantastic to meet God? Why? Why not?

STARTER

A

Wouldn't it be fantastic, and so much easier for people like me who don't really know, if God just came in, sat down here with us and offered me a cigarette or poured me a cup of coffee. Then everyone would know and I could say, 'It's all right. I've seen him. It's fine. Relax. Join in.'

Television comedienne Caroline Quentin, talking to Anglican Bishop Roy Williamson

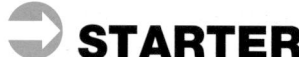

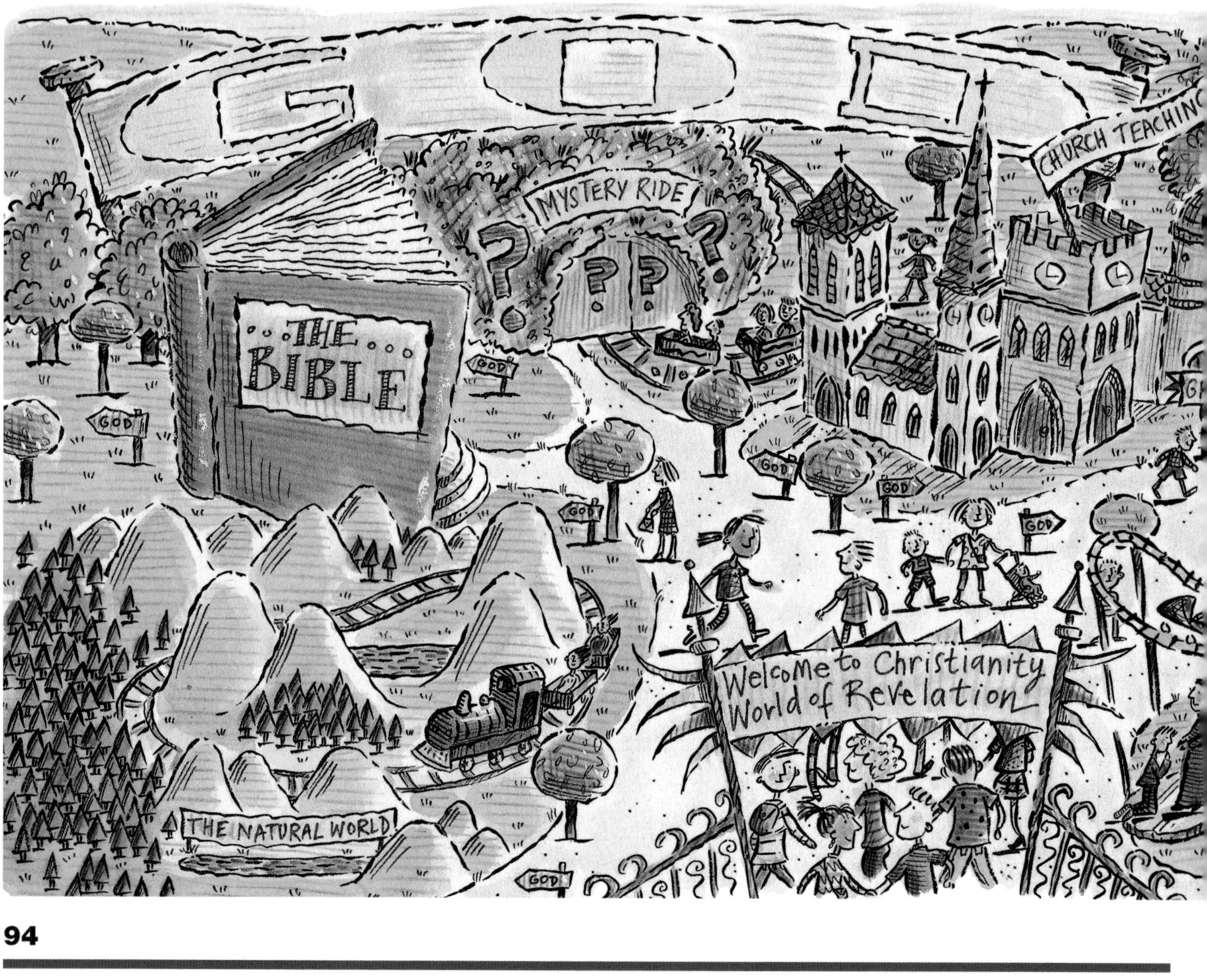

Christians believe that some things about God are revealed through the **natural world**. The Old Testament psalm writers said, 'The Earth proclaims God's glory'. One poet put it like this: 'Every common bush is afire with God'. On page 80 you saw how some Christians interpret God's character through the natural world. However, few Christians would claim this form of revelation is enough on its own. Most Christians agree that nature reveals God but only to the searchers. So where else do the searchers look?

The Bible is the first and most obvious place. It gives the searcher a much clearer image of the Christian God and how this God is different from other gods. It tells the story of God's relationship with humans, from the Earth's Creation to the founding of the Christian Church. It suggests that, far from Christianity being about people searching for God, it is about God searching for people. Christians call this God's SELF-REVELATION.

Some evangelical Christians claim that the Bible is so complete a revelation that it may be all you need. They call the Bible the 'Word of God'. They would say that its words were inspired by God and give so complete a picture of what God is and how God wants people to live that it can be relied on to guide them in any situations in the modern world. If someone now claimed they had a revelation from God they would first test it out to see if fitted in with what the Bible says.

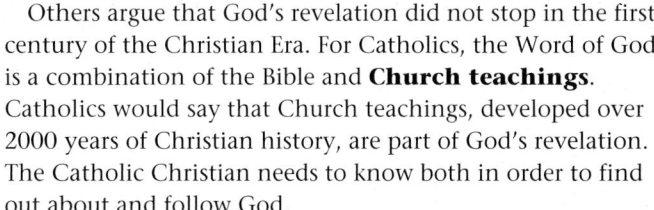

Others argue that God's revelation did not stop in the first century of the Christian Era. For Catholics, the Word of God is a combination of the Bible and **Church teachings**. Catholics would say that Church teachings, developed over 2000 years of Christian history, are part of God's revelation. The Catholic Christian needs to know both in order to find out about and follow God.

These are the two main forms of revelation but there are others.

Some searchers find God is revealed to them through the lives of **great Christians**. These people seem closer to God than ordinary people. They understand more of God, and searchers can meet God through them and learn from their successes and failures. They can copy them and be inspired by them.

Other searchers find God through **Christian worship**. The words of the liturgy (carefully crafted, over centuries, by church leaders) bring them closer to God and tell them what they need to hear about God. Or the rituals, the colours, the smells and the sounds of worship – from the solemnity of the Eucharist (see page 100) to the energy of charismatic worship – help worshippers feel like they are being 'ushered into the presence of God'.

Then underlying all of this is the possibility for all Christians that they themselves, at some time or other, might hear directly from God. Not all Christians do. But most Christians would believe it is very possible that one day God might communicate directly with them. Many Christians have had **personal experiences** when they have felt directly in touch with God. They have heard words spoken as if by God; they have seen prayers answered as if by God; they have been moved emotionally to feel happy or sad, as if moved by God; they have felt loved by God or lost in awe at the presence of God. There are examples on pages 98–99.

So for some people the personal meeting described in Source A may not be so far-fetched.

SAVE AS …

1 Using the text to help you, write a brief description of how each of the following rides can reveal God to Christians:
   a) the natural world
   b) the Bible
   c) Church teachings
   d) religious leaders.
   You can also use examples from earlier in this book.

2 Is God revealed in other ways? What might be in the mystery ride? Write a description of the ride to add to the theme park.

How does religious experience help Christians to know God?

Conversion

Conversion means becoming a follower of God.

The Bible contains spectacular examples of conversion: Moses was called by God from a burning bush (Exodus 3); Saul (Acts 9) was on his way to break up a Christian meeting when he was called by a voice from heaven.

In the modern evangelical tradition, conversion has a special significance. It is seen as the entry point to faith. To be converted is much more important, for example, than being baptised; a person has to admit their sins to God and ask for God's forgiveness. Some evangelicals call this being 'born again' or 'saved'. An important feature at evangelical meetings is often a call for people to come forward and commit their lives to God. However, conversion happens within all traditions. It can result from meditation, prayer or reading.

Some people's conversion is a physical experience. They may cry uncontrollably or feel dizzy or weak at the knees. Some people feel afraid, some indescribably happy. Conversions might coincide with another experience. Sick people have found themselves healed at their conversion (see page 84, for example). Many people find that conversion changes the direction of their lives forever. It changes their relationships with family and friends. For some Christians, conversion is the most important religious experience in their life. They look back to it in later years as the time when God's nature or God's will or God's attitudes were revealed specially to them. They felt that God loved them personally or had a plan for their lives.

B

One dark wintry afternoon I was sitting alone in my study at school. I suddenly became aware of a figure in white whom I saw pretty clearly in my mind's eye. I heard the words, 'Follow me'. Instinctively I knew that this was Jesus. Heaven knows how – I knew nothing about him.

It was an indescribably rich event that filled me afterwards with overpowering joy. I could do no other than follow those instructions.

Extract from the autobiography of Bishop Hugh Montefiore. He was born a Jew and was 16 at the time of this experience. He went on to become an Anglican bishop.

✅ CHECKPOINT

Numinous or Awe and Wonder
In 1917 a scholar called Rudolf Otto used the term numinous to describe religious feelings and experiences, which we sometimes call awe and wonder; the feeling of the presence of something greater than us. The word comes from the Latin word *numen*, which means the might of God. Some people feel it during emotional moments in their lives, such as a wedding, the birth of a child, the death of a loved one. Others feel it when faced with nature's extreme beauty – a stunning sunset, stars on a cloudless night, a view of the sea.

Charismatic worship

Some Christians find that after conversion they have a later experience of 'Baptism in the Spirit'. They feel God's Holy Spirit touching them and changing them. They are set free to worship God in an uninhibited way. They are given spiritual gifts, such as speaking in tongues (other languages or strange sounds), prophesying (receiving messages to pass on to others) or having visions. These spiritual gifts are called charismata and they are a central feature of charismatic worship. When worshippers feel close to God they might sing, pray, dance, hold their arms in the air, laugh, cry or shake uncontrollably. There may be words of knowledge or healings (see page 84). Many find that charismatic worship gives them a new sense of God's presence and power.

In John 14.15–16 Jesus promised his disciples that, when he was taken away from them, he would send another 'Comforter' to them: his Holy Spirit. The first Christians experienced the first baptism in the Holy Spirit on the Day of Pentecost. Charismatic worship was central to the first Christians. It was controversial, even then, and many of the letters of Paul deal with how to use these spiritual gifts correctly (see, for example, 1 Corinthians 12.1–11).

Controversy has surrounded the issue of spiritual gifts ever since. The Pentecostal Church grew out of a revival of this kind of worship. More recently, the Charismatic Movement introduced the use of spiritual gifts into mainstream churches in the 1960s. Some churches rejected charismatic worship, regarding it as mass hysteria whipped up by worship leaders. Others embraced it, believing spiritual gifts were the most basic form of spiritual REVELATION – the way for God to communicate directly with people. They pointed to the example of the earliest Christians. The House Church movement started as people left mainstream denominations for new independent churches where they could hold charismatic worship.

Today, charismatic worship is much more accepted. There is now a strong Charismatic movement within the mainstream Protestant, Catholic and Orthodox traditions.

C

Universal Church of the Kingdom of God, London 1999

Meditation and prayer

Meditation means focusing on God. As Christians focus on God, blocking out all distractions, they receive revelation from God. They may see visions or hear voices.

Meditation can take place anywhere – in a church, in the countryside, at home or school in the middle of a busy day. It can involve reading the Bible, praying or fasting (going without food).

Some meditate by cutting themselves off from other humans. Jesus prayed and meditated in the desert as part of his preparation for his teaching ministry. Dame Julian of Norwich was a 14th-century recluse. She lived alone in a cell meditating on God and offering spiritual advice to people who passed by. In her most famous vision, God showed her a hazelnut in the palm of her hand. It seemed so vulnerable that she asked God how it survived. She was answered: 'It lasts and always will because God loves it.' In the same way, she said, everything exists through the love of God.

In his famous *The Practice of the Presence of God* Brother Lawrence (born 1915) suggested a different approach to meditation. He aimed to focus so totally on whatever he was doing – whether cutting a vegetable or washing dishes – that God was able to speak to him through that activity.

The Quaker denomination builds its weekly services around silent meditation as a group.

'In a meeting, friends gather in silence as seeking souls ... Often, out of that silence is born the message of that meeting, expressed, it may be, by several speakers and yet with a central thought' (*Quaker Faith and Practice*, paragraph 234).

FOCUS TASK

Draw up a table like this:

Experience	Example	What it reveals about God	I think it is illusion or reality because ...

1 Complete the table using the information panels on these two pages.

DISCUSS

2 Churches that emphasise conversion and charismatic worship are among the fastest growing in the UK and worldwide. Why do you think this might be?

Pilgrimage

In September 2003, Sarah Bingham, a charity worker and evangelist from London, set out to walk the 175 miles (300 km) from Leon to Santiago, along the famous PILGRIMAGE route called the Camino. The traditional goal is to walk to the cathedral at Santiago, to see the reliquary of St. James, then on to Finisterre to watch the sun set over the Atlantic at 'the end of the world'.

• Why did you go on a pilgrimage?
I went because it gives time and space to think about God without having to worry about other things. I chose Santiago because I read a book about it in my teens – I'd always wanted to go. From a practical point of view, the route is very well marked and there are pilgrim hostels (refugio) all the way along.

• How many people do this pilgrimage?
Thousands of people do it all year round, but spring and autumn are the best times for walking. Most pilgrims are Catholic. All pilgrims greet each other with 'Buen Camino' (which means 'good road').

• Were you on your own?
I flew out to join a friend who had been walking already for two weeks. But we soon discovered that he and I couldn't walk together because he was too quick for me. So sometimes I walked on my own, and sometimes I walked with other people who did walk the same pace as me, and who stayed at the same refugio as me.

• How did you experience God on your pilgrimage?
In all kinds of ways. I took a book on Christian meditation with me that made helpful suggestions about how to think about God.

I also read a section of the Bible each day. In one village I went into a Catholic church, to find a cool place to read my next chapter of Mark's gospel, and to get a stamp to say that I had reached this place on the pilgrimage. In the church there was a small crucifix on the wall with one of Jesus' hands nailed to the cross and the other reaching down towards the congregation. It reinforced that the whole point of the cross was something Jesus did for all people. The cross is one of God's ways of reaching out to all people and saying, 'Come to me, you are welcome, I love you.'

God also worked through relationships. In the refugio you live very closely with people you don't know. There is a real comradeship. You are all on the same journey to Santiago, looking for God and you are depending on each other.

Centuries ago pilgrimages were all about the end point – people went to visit the shrine of Sant Iago (St James) and when they got there they had to wash at Lavacola, attend mass, kiss the statue of St James and pray. For me it wasn't so much what we were walking to, it was the experiences on the way that made me feel closer to God.

• How has doing the pilgrimage changed you?
It made me a lot more open to hearing God speak to me in different ways – not just from the Bible. It has also sharpened my focus on the fact that western living is far too cluttered and that as Christians we should de-clutter our lives and live much more simply. While I was there I read a statement that stayed with me: 'Pilgrims do not grasp, they are grateful'. I now know that is very true. When I got back to the fast pace of the city I was more determined to spend time 'being with God' and not just 'doing things for God'.

How God is revealed through the Eucharist

At the Eucharist worshippers take bread and wine, called the 'elements'. These are symbols of Jesus' body and blood. The Eucharist is one of the seven sacraments used by Christian Churches. A sacrament is 'an outward sign of an inward grace', which means a ritual to feed Christian faith.

Jesus initiated the Eucharist. He said to his disciples at their last meal together, 'This is my body which is given for you. Do this in memory of me.' (Luke 22.19). The Eucharist is a central feature of worship in the Catholic and Orthodox traditions and in many Protestant churches. It has various other names: Communion, Mass, Lord's Supper, Breaking Bread.

Roman Catholics call the Eucharist the **Mass**. Active Roman Catholics take Mass weekly or even daily. There is a fixed liturgy (words spoken by the priest and congregation) which provides a set pattern for the entire service. Only a priest can bless the bread and wine, and give it to the congregation.

For many Christians the experience of taking the Eucharist is the focus of their religious life. As prayers are said and songs are sung, the bread is given to each individual with the words: 'This is the body of Christ – feed on him in your hearts.' Some worshippers believe the bread and wine become the actual body and blood of Christ. This is called 'transubstantiation'. Others believe the elements are symbols. In either case, the Eucharist celebrates the presence of Christ in the world and in a Christian's life. It is a physical reminder that Jesus is on Earth.

It gains special significance from being an experience shared with millions of other Christians all over the world, from a massive open-air Mass with hundreds of thousands of other Christians to a simple service for the housebound.

A Christian's first Eucharist is a rite of passage. People prepare carefully for it. Those who are not ready to take Communion often come forward for a blessing by the priest – even babies are brought by their parents.

ACTIVITY

A What you can see

Examine Photos D–G.

1 All four photos show a Eucharist service. Discuss with a partner the similarities and differences between these photos. For example look at: the postures; whether children are participating or not; what they are drinking from; what they are eating; where the service is happening; who is giving out the elements.

2 Draw a line across the middle of a piece of paper. Make notes above the line to record all the things that you can see.

B What you can't see

Even more important at the Eucharist is what is going on inside the people – their experience. That is something that you can't see. Read the two accounts opposite and the other information on this page. Then make notes below the line to record what is going on in the heart or mind of the believer at Eucharist.

SAVE AS ...

Add an extra row to your chart from page 99 to record your ideas about Eucharist.

D

Armenian Orthodox communion, Epiphany (6 January)

E

Othona community communion

F

Baptist communion

G

Priest giving communion to elderly people at home

CAS

Richard Tillbrook – Anglican priest

"To me, as a priest, the Eucharist is central to my life and, I am glad to say, it seems to be central to the life of the people who worship with me at my church. We celebrate the Eucharist because Jesus told us to, and the words of consecration which, we believe, only a priest can offer, make the bread and wine the real and actual presence of Jesus Christ in our midst. Of course we know that Jesus is always with us but rather as we might say that our loved ones are always with us it is quite a different thing when they actually appear. We believe Jesus actually joins us at the Eucharist. The words of consecration – 'This **is** my body which is given for you, Do this in remembrance of me' and 'this **is** my blood of the new covenant which was shed for you and for many, for the forgiveness of sins, Do this as often as you drink it, in remembrance of me' – ring absolutely true in our hearts and minds. We believe that the sacrament is very special and we keep some 'reserved' in an aumbry or tabernacle which is specially set aside and has a lamp permanently alight to show us that Jesus is here. We use this reserved bread in emergencies. If someone is ill and needs communion quickly but there isn't time for the priest to consecrate or if there is no priest available, then a 'lay person' can take the sacrament which has been consecrated by a priest, to the sick.

The Eucharist is the greatest form of praise we can offer to God because we are doing exactly what Jesus told us to do. The Eucharist is so important that we feel lost and distressed if we are deprived of it and that is why, in our tradition, it is very common for the priest to visit the homes of people who can't get to church and to bring them the sacrament, bring Jesus if you like, to them.

Some people criticise us and say that having the Eucharist available every day makes it too common and 'familiarity breeds contempt', etc. I can only say that for me and for my people this could not be further from the truth . . . we love God so much that every moment we can grab in his presence is to be treasured. I can only liken it to people who are in love . . . try telling them that they should see less of each other! When you love someone, you just want to be with them and set time aside for them, don't you?

Of course you do . . . and that is how I feel about Jesus in the sacrament of the Eucharist. Of course I have to get on with the work of being a priest in the community but the highlight of the day is spending time . . . real quality time . . . with **Him**."

Claire Clinton – Charismatic Christian

"Breaking Bread to me encompasses so many different emotions ranging from praise, thanksgiving, awe and wonder, to stillness and solemnity. In my church the way we take communion changes every time it takes place – it usually flows out of our worship, so it may end quietly or be a vibrant celebration of all that Jesus saves us from. The words that are used for the actual Breaking Bread are often the same, taken from Jesus' words on the night before his death, or from St Paul when he wrote to some of the early Christian churches to tell them how they should break bread, but nothing else about how it might be done stays the same. I like this, I know people like ritual and tradition staying the same, but I think that if we are to really remember Jesus' death on the cross we need to at times be surprised by God, and look at His death from different angles. Also, historically, Breaking Bread was done in their homes not a church, usually as a part of a shared meal together. So it shouldn't necessarily be a formal or religious ceremony, but rather a way of remembering who we are living for.

Sometimes when I am taking the bread and wine I feel that it is a time just for me and God, and everyone else there at church just slips away – I am there with my saviour and redeemer, telling him how much I love him. At other times it is an act of fellowship that brings me closer to God as well as those I worship with at church. It joins us in a united message and vision for all that God has for us to do in this world. Breaking bread is often an emotional time for me. Thinking about all that Jesus has saved me from, or all that he was prepared to go through to put me back in a right relationship with God, touches me deeply inside.

In my church we celebrate Breaking Bread twice a month on a Sunday morning and once a month in a smaller group that meets for Bible Study. Anyone who loves Jesus as their saviour can take the bread and wine in my church. I have two small children and they eat the bread and drink the wine (usually red grape juice) with my husband and me – it is a time when we can as a family thank Jesus for all that he has done for us. My six-year-old is always keen to say his own prayers to Jesus before he eats the bread and drinks the wine."

CASE STUDY: The Dunblane massacre

The Dunblane massacre, which happened in 1996, was a national tragedy. This cold-blooded, pre-meditated killing touched a nerve throughout Britain. The first reaction, not surprisingly, was shock and horror at 16 innocent lives destroyed. But talk soon turned to 'evil'. A parent at the school said, 'Today we have been visited by evil'. The GCSE students below talked about it too.

E

They were in the school gym when the gunman opened fire. Three minutes later 16 children lay dying

… it seems that the teacher died trying to shield her pupils from the bullets. In his final act, Thomas Hamilton, 43, who was forced to quit the Scouts amid abuse allegations, turned the gun on himself and committed suicide.

F

Anita: His own past experiences put evil in the killer's mind.

Alex: God can bring good into the world – he did so at Creation – but he can't be responsible for evil.

Richard: We all have different emotions – hate, love and so on – they can be used for good or bad. That is how evil gets into the world, it is the way that people use their emotions. To hate my teacher would be wrong, but to hate Hitler is all right because it is a response to his actions.

Felicity: You can't blame the evil in the world on Satan, we have to accept that we have evil in us – it goes back to original sin and free will.

Rohan: If God is pulling the strings for good, then surely Satan is pulling the strings for bad or evil on earth. We choose which we allow to control us.

Helen: We all have an element of badness in us, but it is only when the bad overtakes the good that we start to become evil and sinful.

Extracts from a taped conversation at a school Christian Union meeting the week after the Dunblane massacre. The group included Anglicans, Catholics and Baptists.

ACTIVITY

1 Copy a simplified version of the diagram on the right onto a sheet of A3 paper.
2 Study Source F. Write each student's name on a slip of paper.
3 With a partner, place each slip of paper in an appropriate place on your diagram, according to that student's belief about where evil comes from. You might disagree about where to place them. You might need to adapt the diagram or add new headings.
4 Add your own name in an appropriate place to show what you believe.

SAVE AS …

5 Record in your own words the three different explanations of evil as:

• a person
• a force
• a psychological phenomenon.

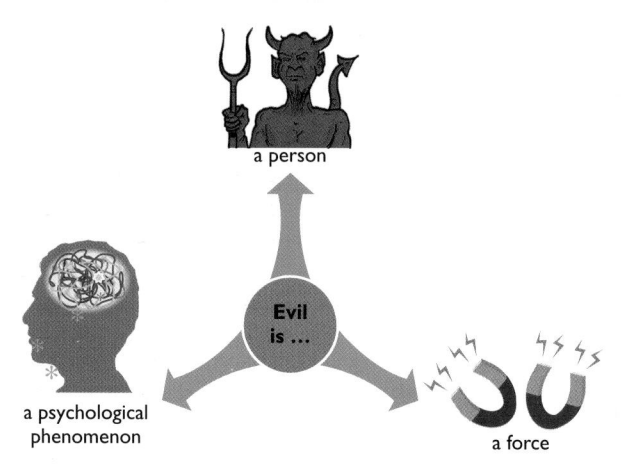

a person

Evil is …

a psychological phenomenon

a force

ACTIVITY

1 On your own copy of the diagram below, write each of quotations 1–7 wherever you think it best belongs.

God will give
you power
to cope.

Don't worry. It's all
part of God's plan.

Suffering will end
one day … in heaven
if not before.

Christian
responses
to evil and
suffering

Jesus has
suffered too.

How you deal with
your suffering could
draw others to God.

Learn from your
suffering. Suffering
strengthens us.

2 Imagine you are making a card for a Christian friend who has suffered in some way (you can decide how). Choose one quotation to use in your card. Say why you have chosen it. If none of the quotations appeals to you, explain why you have rejected them. Write your own message instead.

3 Design an appropriate picture for your card.

SAVE AS …

4 Explain in your own words how suffering can cause a Christian to question:
   a) God's love
   b) God's power.

5 Christians believe there are arguments to counter these doubts. How might a Christian reply to each problem?

1
God sets the time for
sorrow and the time for joy.

Ecclesisates 3.4, part of an
Old Testament poem about
the futility of life

2
My A Level teacher had
muscular dystrophy. His trust in
God was an example to me and
encouraged my own faith.

Sally Lynch,
RE teacher and author

3
Even if I go through the
deepest darkness, I will not be
afraid, Lord, for you are with me.

Psalm 23.4

4
Who fears to suffer cannot
belong to Him who suffered.

Tertullian, 3rd century CE

5
God will wipe away all tears from
their eyes. There will be no more death,
no more grief or crying or pain.

Revelation 21.4, a poetic vision of the end of the world

6
Your pain has a purpose. I can't tell you
what that purpose is – that is something you will
discover in your own walk with God.

John Haggai, 20th century

7
The Christian faith gives hope and purpose
even in apparently hopeless situations. God's
powerful love promises a future, and the
security of continuing care and strength to us
when we have none of our own.

Lis, a Church of England priest and chaplain to a hospice for
terminally-ill children

FOCUS TASK

God is on trial. God is being accused of negligence; of knowing about human suffering and human evil and yet having done nothing to prevent it.

Imagine you have been called to give evidence at a trial. You have to write a speech for either the defence or the prosecution. Your speech should be a maximum of one minute – so you only need to write about half a page. It doesn't need to be polished prose – you can just write bullet points.

Also, you won't be able to cover all the issues so just take one or two points from the unit that you feel strongly about and focus on them.

What lies beyond the grave?

Do you believe in life after death? Many people do although they don't agree what form it might take. In this investigation you will examine what different Christians believe about life after death and compare that with your own beliefs. For your final task you will design a new funeral service to reflect a range of different beliefs.

 **STARTER**

A

I believe that when the body dies, the soul lives on in a new life. It's like when you plant a seed to make a new plant. The new plant is beautiful, but if you dig the seed up you will find it is all rotten and horrible. At Orthodox funerals we place a bowl of grain on a table to remind us of this idea.

Anthony, an Orthodox Christian

B

My church used to teach that when you die you can't go straight to heaven because no one is perfect enough to come into the the the presence of God. So you went to purgatory – a kind of halfway house where you could become perfect and ready to enter heaven itself. We do not hear that so much today, but the idea makes sense to me.

Keith, a Catholic priest in London

C

When my father died I was very sad, but I believe I will meet him one day in heaven. He was a Christian. I feel close to him even now. Every week we say in the Creed 'I believe in the Communion of saints' – that means the togetherness of all Christians, all over the world, living and dead.

Sarah, a teacher and a member of an Anglican church

D

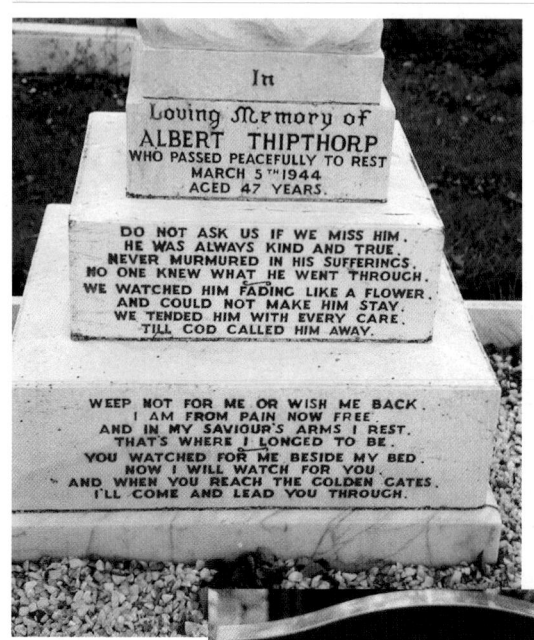

Tombstones in a cemetery in Cambridgeshire

ACTIVITY

Source	What lies beyond the grave?

1 Draw up a table like this, then complete it to show the different beliefs about life after death expressed in Sources A–D.
2 What do they agree about?
3 What do they disagree about?

DISCUSS

4 Discuss with a partner what you believe about life after death. Discuss whether you agree or disagree with the views in your table.

SAVE AS …

5 Write a paragraph recording your own views about life after death.

What happens at a Christian funeral?

(handwritten margin notes: Requiem mass used as part of service to pray for soul of dead person)

Everyone in England and Wales has the right by law to have their funeral service in their parish church or, if they prefer, to have a parish priest take a service at the local crematorium. The vast majority of people in England and Wales choose to have a 'Christian' funeral, whether or not they have attended church during their lives. A funeral is seen as a way of saying goodbye, of coming to terms with the loss of a loved one, and of celebrating their life.

These are the elements you would expect to find in most Christian funerals.

E

	Usually	Sometimes

	• Prayers
	  – for the dead
	  – for the bereaved
	• Bible readings – a favourite one is John 11.17–27
	• A eulogy (talk about the dead person)
		• Hymns – the most common choice is The Lord's My Shepherd (based on Psalm 23)
		• A sermon

	• The commendation – giving the body and soul to God • The committal – lowering the body into the ground or sending the body through a curtain into the cremator	• Sprinkling the coffin with water • Covering the coffin with a pall • Placing a cross on the coffin
	• A final blessing on those present	• Eucharist (or Holy Communion) • Lighting a paschal candle (Easter candle) as a reminder of the resurrection

(handwritten margin notes: Prayers – dead bereaved; Blessing)

F

A funeral is one way of acknowledging that every individual, no matter what they have done in their life, or who they were, is of significance to God. So in a funeral we rejoice in the individuality of a person and the uniqueness of God's creation.

Rev Jonathan Lawson, an Anglican priest

✓ CHECKPOINT

Heaven and hell

A physical heaven

Some Christians think this will be resurrection of the body. They believe that after they die their **body** will rise to life again and be with God in a physical heaven just as happened to Jesus.

A spiritual heaven

Others believe in the immortality of the soul. When people die their **souls** live on. In this view, heaven is not a place but a state of mind.

Judgement

Most Christians also believe in the idea of judgement after death. They see God as a wise judge who understands human actions and motives completely. God will treat people in the afterlife according to their life on Earth. So pleasing God and doing what God wants in this life is one way of ensuring that your life after death is a good one in heaven. The opposite also applies: ignoring God and disobeying God's commands in this life can ensure that your life after death is a bad one in hell.

What about hell?

The Bible is even less specific about hell than it is about heaven, which is one reason why Christians have differing views on the subject. The parable of the rich man and Lazarus (Luke 16.19–31) gives some idea of what early Christians believed happened to the souls of those who had behaved badly.

Some Christians believe strongly in hell and everlasting punishment for those who have committed terrible, violent crimes against others. Others see hell as a spiritual state – eternal separation from God. Still others reject the idea of hell entirely. They argue that God's saving power extends to all people, whatever sins they have committed.

Images of heaven

Although the Bible often mentions heaven it is rarely described. So Christians have differing ideas about heaven.

G

Then I saw a new heaven and a new Earth. The first heaven and the first Earth disappeared, and the sea vanished. And I saw the Holy City, the new Jerusalem, coming down out of heaven from God, prepared and ready, like a bride dressed to meet her husband. I heard a loud voice speaking from the throne: 'Now God's home is with human beings! He will live with them, and they shall be his people. God himself will be with them, and he will be their God. He will wipe away all tears from their eyes. There will be no more death, no more grief or crying or pain. The old things have disappeared.'

Revelation 21.1–4

H

Bring us, O Lord, at our last awakening into the house and gate of heaven, to enter into that gate and dwell in that house where shall be no darkness nor dazzling, but one equal light; no noise nor silence, but one equal music; no fears nor hopes, but one equal possession; no ends nor beginnings, but one equal eternity in the habitations of your glory and dominion, world without end.

John Donne, an English poet (1573–1631)

I

The Coronation of the Virgin by Edward Burra. According to Catholic tradition, the Virgin Mary was taken up to heaven and crowned Queen of heaven.

ACTIVITY

1 Make a list of all the words you associate with 'heaven'.
2 Compare your list with those of others in your class.
3 Which of your ideas can you see in Sources G or H?

Who will go to heaven?

Heaven is God's gift to anyone who believes in Jesus, repents of sin and asks God's forgiveness.

God is a welcoming God. All people, from all religions, will go to heaven.

You can earn your place in heaven by living a good life.

God has already decided who will go to heaven.

Salvation is one of the most controversial topics in Christian theology. Christians would give a wide range of answers if asked, 'Who is saved by God?' or 'Who, if anyone, will go to heaven?' Jesus made it clear that it is not for human beings to judge who will be saved and who will not – only God can make such decisions (see Matthew 7.1-6, for example). Nevertheless, Christians have always discussed this issue. Some of the most common views can be seen on the left.

The significance of Jesus

You can see that what Christians believe about salvation and eternal life is closely related to what they believe about Jesus.

- ❏ Through his life, because he was human, Jesus provides Christians with the perfect example of how they should live.
- ❏ Through his death, because he was God, Jesus could resolve the problem of sin and human failure.
- ❏ Through his resurrection, he conquers death. He shows God's total power over death.
- ❏ Some people also believe that when he returns to Earth he will judge all people as to how well they have followed God. At that point he will divide people into those who have received the gift of eternal life and those who have refused it.

According to the Gospels, Jesus himself said, 'I am the resurrection and the life – no one comes to the Father except through me'. Many Evangelical Christians believe this shows that only Christians who believe in Jesus as the Son of God and as their saviour can go to heaven.

Faith and works

What Christians believe about salvation affects their daily life. It particularly affects their attitude towards the relationship between their beliefs and their actions, or what the New Testamant calls 'faith' and 'works'. If people believe that their faith in Jesus is what saves them, they might see no need to lead a good life. If they believe that their actions are what saves them, they may think that beliefs do not matter. Most Christians believe it is important to combine the two – leading a good life as well as believing in Jesus.

FOCUS TASK

In recent years the Church of England has reviewed all its services, funeral services included. The funeral service is now very flexible. Priests can take into account the varying wishes of the family in designing a service.

1 Working in groups you are going to design a funeral service to reflect what you believe about life after death. You can include as much or as little of the typical Christian funeral as you wish. It should include at least one reading, some music, and some words

for the people at the funeral to say together. You can present it how you wish – as a booklet, a service sheet or a diagram.

2 When you have designed your service write two paragraphs of evaluation.

Paragraph 1: explain what you were trying to achieve in your service and how well you feel you have achieved it.

Paragraph 2: explain what Christians would like or dislike about your service. Would a Christian want to add or change anything? If so what would they change and how would they change it?

Conclusion

Your exam

Your chief concern is probably to get a good grade in your exam. We have helped you in various ways. Here is a reminder of the ideas you will need to bear in mind when you revise for your exam.

Different traditions

Christians have a range of views. There is no one single, unified Christian opinion. In your exam, you will need to show that you understand this and that you are aware of the way Christian traditions take different attitudes to moral and theological issues.

You will improve your grade if you can show your grasp of the differences between Christian traditions, or between Christianity and another religion, on moral issues.

Sources of authority

You have examined the ways Christians use sources such as the Bible or their church leaders as authorities.

You will improve your grade if you can show not only the sources of authority used by different Christians, but also how they use each source of authority.

Absolute and relative

You have investigated the difference between an absolutist approach to morality and a relativist approach and have recorded your own examples of absolutist and relativist responses to different issues.

You will improve your grade if you can refer to absolutist and relativist morality confidently. You should show you understand that they are not watertight definitions; rather, they show an 'approach' to decision-making on certain issues by certain traditions.

Core beliefs

You have studied some of the core beliefs that lie at the heart of Christian thinking on moral issues, such as stewardship and the sanctity of life.

You will improve your grade if you can not only describe such beliefs, but also demonstrate how these beliefs inspire Christians and affect their values and their actions. Christianity is a living faith, evolving and changing year by year as its followers meet new challenges. The course is about real-life Christianity. It is your understanding of the relationship between these beliefs and Christian values and actions that will interest the examiner.

Your own views

This course has given you plenty of opportunity to express your own views and to give reasons for them. You may be surprised that even this will be useful in your exam.

Sometimes you are specifically asked for your view in an exam question. The **reasons** for your opinion, and your ability to back it up, interest the examiner more than the viewpoint itself. So, remember: you will improve your grade if you can express your own views on issues you have tackled, and explain and support them with reference to the Christian ideas you have studied in this book.

Your beliefs and values

One of the aims of Religious Education is to learn from religion. Religion gives its followers beliefs and values to live by. This course has encouraged you to debate, to understand and to make your own decisions about Christian beliefs and values. The beliefs and values you have studied in this course may be similar to your own or they may be different. In either case, this course should have helped you to clarify your own beliefs and values.

FOCUS TASK

The illustration shows some values that Christians might think were important to help guide people in their moral decision-making.

1 Choose three that you would like to take with you into the future. Explain your choice.
2 Explain whether you reject any of the values altogether and, if so, why.
3 For your three chosen values, draw a diagram showing how your values might affect your beliefs or your actions in the future.

Glossary

ABSOLUTE MORALITY belief that there is a right course of action that is true for all situations

ACTIVE EUTHANASIA something done to hasten death such as drug doses

AGNOSTIC someone who thinks we cannot know whether there is a god

ASSISTED SUICIDE helping someone to perform their own euthanasia

ATHEIST someone who believes there isn't a God

BAPTIST a branch of the Protestant Church that practises adult baptism by total immersion

CATHOLIC a branch of Christianity that emphasises the Pope's authority

CHARISMATA spiritual gifts such as speaking in tongues or having visions

COMPULSORY/INVOLUNTARY EUTHANASIA ending the life of someone ill, as decided by other people such as doctors or relatives

COSMOLOGICAL ARGUMENT an argument that God must exist because the universe must have come from somewhere: from God

DISCRIMINATION treating someone unfairly based on prejudice; an action

EUCHARIST Holy Communion

EVANGELICAL describes Christians who believe that the Bible is the word of God and that believers should make a public statement about their faith

GENERAL REVELATION revelation that is indirect and available to everyone, such as nature

HOSPICE a home for people who are ill, often terminally, usually run by religious people

IMMANENT in the world

LIBERAL describes Christians who believe that the Church must change over time and that the Bible can be interpreted for modern life although it is not all literally true

LIBERATION THEOLOGY a theory that says Christians should get involved in politics and attempt to free people from social, political and economic oppression

NUMINOUS indicating the presence of God

ORTHODOX a branch of Christianity that emphasises the mystery of God

PASSIVE EUTHANASIA treatment withdrawn to hasten death such as withdrawal of feeding tube

PILGRIMAGE a spiritual journey to a place of worship

PREJUDICE an opinion that is not based on fact; an attitude

PROTESTANT a branch of Christianity that emphasises the authority of the Bible

RELATIVE MORALITY belief that the right course of action depends on the circumstances of individual situations

REVELATION the way that God communicates with people

SACRAMENTS an outward sign of an inward grace; a Christian ritual such as the Eucharist

SANCTITY OF LIFE belief that life is holy or sacred

SPECIAL REVELATION revelation that is direct to an individual or group, such as a vision

TELEOLOGICAL ARGUMENT an argument that God must exist because of the design of the natural world: God must have designed it

THEIST someone who believes there is a God

TRANSCENDENT beyond the world

VOLUNTARY EUTHANASIA ending the life of someone who has requested it

Index